American Clocks
for the Collector

By the same author

European Clocks
Craft of the Clockmaker
Clocks and Watches
Black Forest Clocks

American
Clocks
for the
Collector

by
E. J. TYLER

E. P. DUTTON

NEW YORK

*First published 1981, in the United States of America
by E. P. Dutton, Inc.,
2 Park Avenue, New York, NY 10016.*

ISBN 0-525-93212-7 (cloth)
ISBN 0-525-47682-2 (DP)

10 9 8 7 6 5 4 3 2 1 First Edition

The illustrations on pages i and iii
are reproduced from the 1880 catalogue
issued by the Ansonia Clock Company,
by courtesy of the American Clock & Watch
Museum, Inc., Bristol, Connecticut.

Printed in Great Britain by BAS Printers Limited,
Over Wallop, Hampshire

Contents

Black-and-white illustrations   vii
Colour plates   xi
Acknowledgements   xiii

1 The Earliest American Clocks   1
     Colonial and Revolutionary Clocks   1
     The Arrival of Mass Production   9
     Collectors' Items   19

2 The OG   23
     Jerome's OG   23
     OG Variations   27
     Clockpapers and Other Means of Dating   32
     Preserving the OG   36

3 The Mainspring   38
     Mainspring Pioneers   40
     Fusees and Direct Drive   46

4 The Later Spring Clocks   53
     Ansonia Clocks and others   54
     Welch, Spring & Co   60
     Wall Clocks   63
     Marketing, at Home and Abroad   68

5 The Balance Clocks   71
     Portable Clocks   71
     Alarms, Drums and Novelties   77

6 Off the Beaten Track   87
     The Calendar Clock   90
     Inventors and their Patents   96

7 Imitations and Reproductions   105
     German Imitations   106
     British Importers and Casers   111
     British Imitations   117
     American Imitations   119

8   Repairs   122
   Repairing Wooden Movements   123
   Repairing Metal Movements: the OG   127
   Re-assembly: the OG   134
   Repairing Other Clocks   141

9   The Restoration of Cases and Dials   145
   The Case   145
   The Dial   150
   The Hands   154
   The Label   156

10   Collecting and the Collector   159
   Clock Societies   159
   Studying Clocks   162
   Reproductions   165
   Kits and Materials   168

Bibliography   172
Appendix I   Clock Papers   181
Appendix II   Export to Britain   186
Appendix III   Makers and Suppliers   191
Appendix IV   The State of Connecticut   197
Appendix V   The Ansonia Factory, New York   198
Appendix VI   Sam Slick   204
Index   206

Black-and-white Illustrations

A Case on Case clock by David Wood, *c.* 1815   5
A Banjo clock by Simon Willard, *c.* 1805   7
A wooden hang-up movement   11
Eli Terry's first shelf clock, made by Seth Thomas, *c.* 1816   12
A Terry-type shelf-clock movement   14–15
A carved-column shelf clock, *c.* 1830   17
An eight-day brass-movement clock from the Forestville
    Manufacturing Company, 1835–9   17
The dial from a clock by Gideon Roberts, *c.* 1800   20
A Tall or Long Case clock by Seth Youngs, *c.* 1745   20
An OG with alarm mechanism by Chauncey Jerome, 1840–45   22
The Brewster single-pin strike movement   28
An eight-day column clock by Birge & Fuller, 1844–8   28
The difference between the Brewster single-pin strike and the
    normal method of striking as used in an OG   29
A miniature OG by Jerome & Co   36
A miniature wall clock by Seth Thomas   36
An early method of using a leaf-spring, by Joseph Ives   41
An eight-day Beehive by Brewster & Ingrahams, 1844–52   42
The movement of the Brewster & Ingrahams clock stripped down   43
The movement of a Brewster & Ingrahams thirty-hour Sharp
    Gothic   44
The original design of the Brewster & Ingrahams Sharp Gothic
    case   44
A Brewster & Ingrahams Sharp Gothic thirty-hour clock   45
A thirty-hour fusee brass-movement clock in an 'Acorn' case
    by J. C. Brown, *c.* 1850   49
A thirty-hour Wagon Spring by Birge & Fuller, 1844–7   49
A Sharp Gothic alarm by Jerome & Co   52
An eight-day Sharp Gothic from the Ansonia Brass Company,
    1854–69   55
An Ansonia iron-cased clock with the famous 1882 movement   57
A late movement with rack-strike by the Waterbury Clock
    Company   57
A Crystal Regulator by Ansonia, *c.* 1900   59
A mantel clock by Welch, Spring & Co, *c.* 1880   61
The 'Patti' by Welch, Spring & Co, 1880 catalogue   61

The movement of a miniature wall clock by Seth Thomas, after
    1869   63
An Ansonia 12-inch dial   63
An eight-day Beehive movement by Jerome & Co   64
A small timepiece by the William Gilbert Clock Company, *c*.1890   67
An Ansonia eight-day visible-escapement movement in a Royal
    Bonn porcelain case, *c*. 1904   67
Illustrations of carriage and balance clocks from Ansonia's
    1880 catalogue   70
The circular version of the 'Marine or Locomotive', New Haven
    Clock Company, late-nineteenth century   75
A 'Marine or Locomotive', *c*. 1870   75
A Seth Thomas alarm in a bronze case   78
A small Waterbury clock cased to be used as a watch   81
The wheels from a Westclox movement   83
The Seth Thomas 'Joker', post 1879   85
A 'Joker' variation, the 'Student', *c*. 1904   85
Two 'Swingers' from Ansonia's 1880 catalogue   86
A small Gilbert alarm with apparently no unusual features   88
The arrangement on S. B. Terry's principle   88
A Seth Thomas calendar clock   91
A pair of small timepieces by E. N. Welch, 1870s   92
Two versions of the Gale Calendar clock from Welch's 1880
    catalogue   93
The famous Seth Thomas No 2 Regulator, from the 1863
    catalogue   95
Three variations of the Kroeber pendulum   98
New Haven's 'Clyde', a 'Walnut' with a Kroeber pendulum   100
A Briggs rotary-pendulum clock from the E. N. Welch
    Company, 1870s   100
A Waterbury alarm with the winding-hole at XI   103
A 'Marine' type, probably by Junghans, Schramberg   107
An OG by Junghans   107
An American-style timepiece-movement by Philipp Haas
    & Söhne   109
Drop-dials in English-made cases   112
A Beehive clock from the Eagle Manufacturing Company   113
A column-and-mirror-style Holloway   114
A large Holloway Cottage clock   114
A Holloway walnut-cased clock   115

A later Holloway clock with a typical banded case   116
The Fattorini alarm clock   117
Pieces of a wooden hang-up movement   125
Shifting a pinion to avoid the worn part of the leaves   131
Inserting new teeth in wooden and brass wheels   133
A special stake for rebushing pallets   135
Complete pallets   135
Pallets with an extra piece of brass fastened inside   135
The crutch wire before riveting into the steel strip   135
The three stages in making a pendulum-rod   138
The bob hooked on to the end of the pendulum wire   138
Spare pendulum-bobs and pallets   139
A temporary pin   142
The plate for a BUCC movement; a spare Great Wheel for
    an OG; an Ansonia key and normal key; a barrel arbor
    with brass surround; two crank-keys for OGs   144
A Seth Thomas OG as found and after restoration   146
An Ingraham 'Oak' as found   147
A Brewster & Ingrahams OG damaged by fire and partly
    restored   147
An E. N. Welch Beehive as found   148
A selection of spare dials for late-nineteenth-century
    American clocks   150
Setting out a new dial   151
'ST' hands for Seth Thomas clocks   154
A selection of hands   155
A pair of Seth Thomas clocks showing the 'ST' hands   155
A reproduction of the Briggs rotary-pendulum clock   158
A reproduction of Dungan's Mouse clock   163
A reproduction Plato clock   163
A reproduction Ignatz clock   163
A reproduction of Howard's 'Figure of Eight' clock   167
A reproduction Banjo clock   167
A reproduction Girandole   169
OG labels by Chauncey Jerome   182
A Jerome & Co label of the late-nineteenth century   183
The label of a Waterbury thirty-hour Cottage clock   183
An OG of the Forestville Clock Company, 1850, with motto   185
A Beehive from Gilbert, possibly pre 1870   185
Ansonia and British United Clock Company trademarks   191

The Holloway & Co trademark   192
The Jerome and New Haven trademarks   193
The Seth Thomas and Waterbury trademarks   194
The E. N. Welch and Western Clock Manufacturing Company
    trademarks   195
Map of the clockmaking towns of Connecticut   196
The famous Ansonia movement of 1882   199

Colour Plates

facing page

1 Pillar and Scroll Shelf clock. Eli and Samuel Terry,
        1825–29   18
2 Movement of Eli and Samuel Terry Pillar and Scroll   18
3 Long Case, *c.* 1820. Note the inlay is more elaborate
        than on a typical British clock of this period   19
4 Eight-day Column clock by Birge Peck and Co. Bristol,
        Conn., 1849–59. The strap movement used by this
        firm suggests that the clocks are older than they
        really are   34
5 OG by Seth Thomas   35
6 Brewster and Ingrahams eight-day OG with
        Continental-style tablet   35
7 Thirty-hour Column clock by Seth Thomas   35
8 Jerome Octagon Prize Model eight-day, *c.* 1870   66
9 Ansonia Cabinet Clock Peak Model eight-day, *c.* 1880–
        1900   66
10 Ansonia thirty-day Round Head Office Regulator,
        c. 1900   67
11 Ansonia Queen Elizabeth Regulator eight-day, *c.* 1900 67
12 One-day Cottage Striking clock by Waterbury Clock Co.,
        and Sharp Gothic alarm by Ansonia Brass and Copper
        Co., 1869–78   82
13, 14 Sharp Gothics by Jerome, (*left*) thirty-hour striking and
        (*right*) timepiece, both *c.* 1880   83
15 Thirty-hour Beehive by E. N. Welch   83
16 Three German Shelf clocks. Left Philipp Haas & Söhne;
        centre and right, Junghans   114
17 OG by Junghans, grained case not veneered and typical
        Continental-style tablet   114
18 Three German Cottage clocks. That on the left Union
        Clock Co. Others anonymous   115
19 Miniature OG with Continental-type tablet that suggests
        Holloway and Co., yet the clock has an original paper
        of E. N. Welch   115
20, 21 A tablet from an OG by E. N. Welch, *c.* 1870 and
        modern version   130

xii   American Clocks for the Collector   *facing page*

22   A modern pictorial tablet   131

CREDITS

Nos 8–11 are from photographs by Michael Manifold Photography; the remainder by K. N. Crowe.

Acknowledgements

Such a book as this cannot be written without a great deal of assistance, and I would like to thank all those friends who have contributed ideas and made helpful criticisms while it was being written.

Mr Peter Abery
Mr Charles Allix
Mr E. Andrew
Mr Chris Bailey of the
    American Clock and Watch
    Museum, who also supplied
    some of the illustrations
Mr Keith Dachler
Mr Eric Fasey
Mr Andrew Fayle
Mr Bill Matthews

Mr Brian Pearson
Mr Kenneth D. Roberts
Dr F. G. A. Shenton
Mrs R. K. Shenton
Mr Robert Street
Mr Charles Terwilliger
Mr Stacy B. C. Wood Jr.,
    Administrator NAWCC

I should also like to express appreciation of the assistance I have received from Messrs Littlechild and Restall of my publishers and thank Mr Kenneth Crowe for his excellent photographs. The owners of the clocks photographed must also be thanked for their co-operation but regretfully they must remain anonymous.

E. J. Tyler
July 1980

Illustrations supplied by Chris Bailey and the American Clock and Watch Museum, Bristol, Connecticut, on the following pages: 5, 7, 12, 17 (left), 20 (both), 49 (both), 61 (right), 70 (all), 86, 93 (both), 95.

1 The Earliest American Clocks

Clock-collecting as a hobby has been popular for only about the last forty years. Before that time, a limited number of people assembled collections of clocks, but in practically every case the collection consisted of works by London makers, where British collectors were concerned, or pieces belonging to the collector's own country on the Continent. The very limited numbers of collectors in America would collect Continental or British pieces according to taste, but the theme of the collection was almost always from the artistic point of view, and movements were neither understood nor cared about. In the days before 1939, clocks by well-known London makers could be obtained for prices that seem fantastically low when compared with those of today, and no one cared about the simpler types of clock that were widely used in both town and country. In both Britain and America, when a household clock went wrong, it was consigned to the woodshed or the attic and a replacement bought; on the Continent the replacement would be bought, but the clock would be thrown away. We therefore find that large numbers of collectors from overseas are visiting Britain to purchase old clocks, which are disappearing to the Continent and to America. Within the last decade or so, American collectors have been taking home with them some of the many thousands of factory-made clocks that crossed the Atlantic a century ago. The older types of American clock have mostly remained in their own country.

COLONIAL AND REVOLUTIONARY CLOCKS

The story of the American clock is a fascinating one, for, beginning with typically British models, the design was modified out of all recognition by the influence of clockmakers from the Continent and also through difficulties in obtaining raw material. Problems connected with raw material had a great influence on industrial development in America, and the fact that the country began its life as an independent nation comparatively late in history meant that there were no deep-rooted traditions to be overcome.

The first settlement in North America that lasted was that founded in Plymouth by the Pilgrim Fathers in 1620. Many other places were settled during the early-seventeenth century, and life was of the most primitive kind with no luxuries and all kinds of hardships to endure. It is unlikely that there would have been many clocks at this period. Clocks were still comparatively rare in Britain and, up to the end of the sixteenth century, had all been imported from the Continent or made by foreign workmen living in the country. The church clock would have told the time for the town or village, and remote places would have relied on the position of the sun in the sky for the time. With the establishment of new colonies, a clock would have been one of the last things to be thought of. They were extremely expensive and would have had to be imported from Britain.

The standard clock of the early-seventeenth century, which was the first type to have been made by British workmen, was the lantern clock, constructed largely of brass and driven by weights. The timekeeping was controlled by a wheel-balance. After the application of the pendulum to clockwork in 1657 and with the desire to throw off the austerity of the Commonwealth period after the Restoration, clock fashions changed abruptly, and the lantern clock was replaced by more sophisticated designs as far as London makers were concerned. Country makers still produced it, however, and applied the new pendulum to it, first in the short form with verge escapement and later much longer with an anchor escapement.

By the time of Charles II, the colonies in America were well established, and large numbers of people were emigrating to them, mainly for religious liberty. Many clockmakers had now been trained, and the idea of possessing a clock was not so remote as it had been earlier in the century. Clockmakers themselves were among the emigrants, and one of the earliest of whom we have record is Abel Cottey of Crediton, Devon. A clock by him is in the Royal Albert Museum, Exeter, and although this clock has been altered, it gives a good idea of what the earliest type of clock used in the colonies would have looked like. It is a lantern clock with comparatively large wheels and very solidly made.

Most of the eastern colonies were established before the seventeenth century came to an end. The last one was Georgia, which dates from 1733. Thirty years later, when the discontent which was to result in the Declaration of Independence had already begun to appear, the population was sufficiently large and had created enough wealth to render clocks much more common than they had been. The prevailing type was the weight-driven long-case clock in both its eight-day and thirty-hour form, as springs had to be imported and a spring clock of the period needing a fusee was much more difficult and expensive to make. Some of the clocks made in America were quite primitive, but others were up to the standard of those being made in Europe.

Thomas Harland, who emigrated to America in 1773, put an advertisement in the local paper at Norwich, Connecticut, informing the public of what he could do. He offered watches in gold, silver and metal cases, including watches with the horizontal (cylinder) escapement and also repeating-work, spring, musical and plain clocks, church clocks etc, and offered to clean and repair existing clocks and watches. He also offered to cut wheels and fusees for the trade as well as to engrave dials.

At the time of Harland's arrival it is not likely that he would have been called upon to do many of the things he offered. He would have been chiefly in demand for repairs to existing clocks as new ones were expensive, and consequently clocks for the pre-1770 period are rare and therefore in demand with American collectors. They do not frequently change hands.

In later years Harland's business was to prosper, and he had a number of people working for him, but soon after his arrival in America the War of Independence broke out, and for several years the business of clockmaking was interrupted as the clockmakers were either on active service or providing weapons and other equipment. Lead clock-weights were melted down for bullets, as a shortage of metal had always been a problem in the colonies. After the war was over (1782), it took some time for things to settle down, and the acquisition of a clock was not an item of priority with the majority of families.

A development of the post-war period was that clockmakers began to get supplies of rough material from specialist craftsmen instead of making every part themselves. By giving up brass-casting and forging of iron, a lot of time could be saved, and production could be increased to meet the greater demand that slowly arose as the country settled down again. Thomas Harland not only produced clocks himself but was also providing training for other men who subsequently established their own businesses. The most famous of these was Daniel Burnap, whose own apprentice Eli Terry was to revolutionize the horological trade in America.

Burnap was a skilled man who did all kinds of repair work, not only to watches and clocks but also to numerous small objects in metal. He also worked as a silversmith. He has left behind a number of long-case chiming and musical clocks as well as the ordinary hour-strike variety, and these possess dials which he engraved himself. No examples are known outside America, and those in their own country command high prices at sales.

Burnap's shop records have been preserved, together with a number of tools, and have been described in a book which gives a fascinating picture of the work of a clockmaker in America in the late-eighteenth century. (See bibliography: Penrose R. Hoopes, *The Shop Records of Daniel Burnap.*)

One of the largest problems confronting the American clockmaker was the shortage of metal. Secondhand metal was salvaged where possible, but the British type of long-case movement required a good deal of brass in its making. As time went on, complete movements were imported from Britain, and when this occurred, they often had the pillar at the two o'clock position inset, and the American importer would saw off the corner of the plate to give him an extra piece of brass for the workshop. When one sees an eight-day long-case movement in Britain with an inset pillar in this position, it is a good inference that the firm that produced it regularly exported to America. The setting-in of the pillar is a good feature, as it makes the frame stronger, and as no piece of the mechanism is located in this position, the space is available to re-site the pillar without any drastic alterations.

On account of the shortage of metal, an attempt was made to produce something that required less raw material. Weight-drive was retained on account of the difficulty and expense of obtaining springs, but the movement was made smaller and in many instances striking-work was omitted. In order to suggest the more expensive spring clock, a new type of case was produced that resembled a spring clock standing on a small cabinet, although both parts formed one unit. The smaller movement needed less fall for the weight, and by arranging for a heavy weight to fall through a small distance, the overall size was limited. This in its turn meant that the wheelwork had to be of good quality in order to transmit evenly the limited power that is a result of the system.

The type was given the name 'Case on Case', and some fine examples were made, particularly in Massachusetts. While striking was rare, some clocks had a one-at-the-hour strike operated from the

A Case on Case clock
by David Wood,
Newburyport,
Massachusetts,
c. 1815. An eight-day
brass timepiece-
movement in a
mahogany case, with
the name on reverse-
painted glass.

going-train, and even alarm-work was fitted in some instances. Dials could be silvered or painted, but the typical brass dial with silvered chapter-ring that was a feature of pre-Revolutionary long-case clocks is scarcely known on the Case-on-Case type. An unusual feature seen on these clocks is a concave dial, and in a number of them the so-called kidney-shaped dial was provided. The finish of the cabinet-work was generally superb, and there is a suggestion of French influence in treating the clock case more as an article of furniture.

The State of New Hampshire also produced examples of the Case-on-Case clock as well as scaled-down versions of the long-case clock now called 'Grandmother'. The speciality of the State was, however, a clock which hung on the wall with a very shallow case and incorporated a mirror in the front. The mirror was the most prominent feature of the clock, and usually the dial was quite small and placed well to the top. New Hampshire mirror-clocks often have movements with plates of a very unusual shape, a good example of what the American clockmaker was forced to do by having only odd scraps of metal to work with. On some clocks the train is almost horizontal instead of vertical, and even the pallets lie on their side. Striking-work is seen in mirror-clocks, and there is more room for the weights, but the feature of small barrels with large main wheels is still retained to allow the clock to go for the longest time with the shortest drop possible.

A speciality of the mirror-clocks is a system of striking known as 'the Rat Trap'. Here the rim of the great wheel is used as a count-wheel, and instead of having slots or pins, a number of holes are drilled in the rim of the wheel at varying intervals corresponding to the increased number of strokes each hour. When striking is in progress, a wire taps on the face of the rim each time a blow is sounded on the bell, and when the wire meets a hole, it enters it and the train is locked. The system is not particularly reliable, but it uses few parts and therefore less metal. It is a forerunner of the many novel mechanisms that were to appear in connection with American clockmaking once the factory system had been established.

The clock which is most highly prized by collectors in America is the 'Banjo'. The design was produced by Simon Willard of Roxbury, Massachusetts, and was an attempt to produce a weight-driven clock having the delicacy of a spring-driven one and yet being a serviceable and sturdy timekeeper. Willard must have worked out the design

A Banjo Clock by Simon Willard, Boston, Massachusetts, *c.* 1805, original glass retouched; gilt acorn finial.

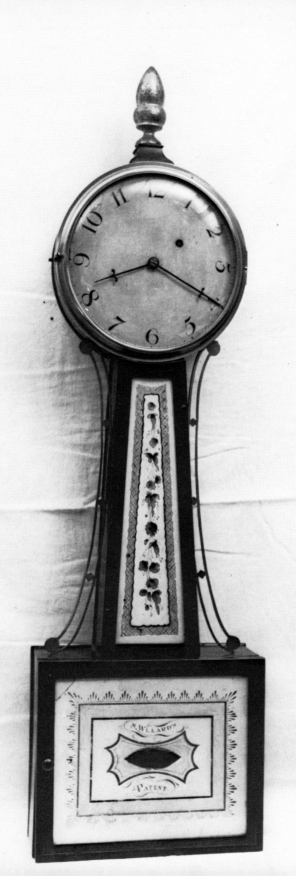

somewhere in the 1790s, but in 1801 the clock was patented and was made by a number of clockmakers for many years afterwards. The Willard design made the clock as slender as possible and saved space by bringing the pendulum and crutch to the front just behind the dial, causing the crutch and pendulum to need a loop for clearing the tubes carrying the hands. The case was in three parts, the top being circular and much the same size as the dial, which was 7 inches in diameter. The middle section was tapered and the bottom rectangular to allow the pendulum-bob to swing. Willard's patent mentions leaving a hole in the colouring of the glass at the lower part to allow the bob to be visible. The principle of a heavy weight falling through a small distance was retained to keep the case small, and the barrel was of small diameter compared with the main wheel. A further saving of space was effected by locating the barrel-arbor in the two o'clock position, thus providing more room for the weight to fall. This was also a feature of the Case-on-Case type, but the problem was more critical in Willard's design.

The clock was a timepiece only, and the movement was very tiny compared with a normal eight-day long-case movement. Later variations included striking-work in some instances, but this was contrary to the original spirit of the design. A case variation known as the 'Lyre' and also an elaboration of the scheme known as the 'Girandole' were further modifications to the original design but cannot be considered improvements. In the mid-nineteenth century the Howard Company of Boston produced a simplified version of the Banjo clock in wooden cases and in several different sizes for use in homes, offices, public rooms etc, and while the ornate appearance of the original was changed for something more functional, the basic idea was retained. (The design was so successful that the same firm is now making reproductions. A London firm is also making reproductions of Banjo clocks but taking the original presentation as the prototype.)

The miniature long-case or 'Grandmother' was made in other states as well as New Hampshire, but there were not a large number of them made and they are highly prized by collectors today. The original style of long-case clock was still produced, although dials and movements were imported from Birmingham, England, and rough material was also imported to make local production easier. When dials of American long-case clocks are found with designs incorporating the Eagle and the Stars and Stripes, this is a good but not necessarily infallible indication of a locally produced dial. During the period 1800–1820 Arabic figures were popular, but the style of the figures used on American dials was different from that used in Britain. The fashion probably originated in France during the Louis XVI period and was seen not only in Britain and America but on the European Continent as well.

In the early years of the nineteenth century the whole system of importation was upset by the Jefferson embargo which prohibited imports into the USA. The motive was political, to make the British Government respect the rights of American shipping, but in practice it did harm to everyone concerned, manufacturers, merchants and craftsmen, and in 1809 the embargo was repealed. Many Americans had ignored it and continued to import goods even though the American Government had given extra powers of search to Revenue Collectors. New England in particular was very much opposed to the embargo. After the Act was repealed, affairs between Britain and America became worse, culminating in the War of 1812 which was not concluded till 1815.

THE ARRIVAL OF MASS PRODUCTION

The international events of this period overshadowed something that was going on in the State of Connecticut at the time and which would affect not only the clockmaking business but also other businesses in the future.

Eli Terry was born in East Windsor, Connecticut in 1772 and was apprenticed to Daniel Burnap, who gave him training in traditional clockmaking which was completed in 1793. The standard clock of the period was the long-case clock, but many of these had wooden movements instead of brass ones not only because of the cheapness but also because metal was in short supply. Terry therefore grew up in a country where a wooden clock was as natural an object as a brass one, unlike many other countries where wooden clocks were comparatively unknown. Other regions where wooden clocks were made were the Black Forest in Germany and some of the villages in Switzerland, but elsewhere wooden clocks were very much in the minority.

Terry established himself in the parish of Northbury in 1795, and shortly afterwards the town of Plymouth was incorporated out of the parish. He began making wooden clock-movements by hand as one-off jobs and then began using machinery and water power. Up to this time all clocks had been made individually, but Terry got the idea of producing them in batches. The scheme had been tried by Eli Whitney for making muskets, when he signed a contract in 1789 with the US Government for four thousand to be delivered in eighteen months and for six thousand more to follow in a year. Whitney took eight years to fulfil his order, but the idea had been established.

Terry was not the only man who thought of making clocks in batches. Gideon Roberts of Bristol, Connecticut, used to make three or four at a time, but he eventually had to give way under competition from Terry's machinery. Terry would go out selling the clocks he made, but he eventually came to the conclusion that it was more profitable to concentrate on production and have someone else do the marketing.

In 1807, possibly as a result of Napoleon's Berlin decree cutting off American commerce from Europe, two partners, Edward and Levi Porter, got the idea that they could sell four thousand clock-movements if they could only buy them cheaply enough. They approached Terry and offered to supply all the material if he would do the work. The price offered was $4 each, about one-sixth of what Terry usually got for a movement, but the idea appealed to him, and he sold his mill and purchased a larger one. For a year he produced no clocks but planned and made the necessary machinery. By 1808 Terry was ready to begin production and started on a batch of five hundred clocks. By the end of the year he had finished them and also as many again. He was joined by a carpenter and joiner named Seth Thomas, whose job at first was to assemble the piles of parts into movements and get them running. In 1809 he was joined by Silas Hoadley, and in 1810 Terry sold the mill to Thomas and Hoadley, who went on producing clocks as before.

By 1810 the clock business was beginning to be well established, and more than ten thousand were made in that year. The inevitable result was a flooded market, and Terry probably realized this. In 1813 Seth Thomas left Silas Hoadley and established himself in a shop in Plymouth Hollow.

The wooden hang-up movements that Terry was producing were often made with pull-up wind, although dummy winding-holes would be painted on the dial for the sake of appearance. Sometimes there were divisions on the barrels to separate the winding-cords

A wooden hang-up movement. Left: With the motion-work outside the front plate. Right: The rear side, showing the count-wheel. Note the way the teeth of the train-wheels lean forward.

from the driving-cords. They were also at a disadvantage in that their hands were made of pewter and that, if they were adjusted in the usual manner, there was a danger of bending them. The way to adjust the time on one of these clocks was to feel behind the dial for the motion-wheels and then turn them with the fingers until the hands showed the correct time. The pewter hands were based on the typical long-case design which was usually made of steel, and a source of material was old drinking-vessels and plates which could be melted down and recast. A pair of hands from an existing clock could provide the pattern for making the mould.

Terry had new plans. The clocks he had been making were simply movements, and the purchaser had to make his own arrangements about a case. Terry's next idea was to produce a movement and case as well and also make the clock much smaller while still using a wooden movement. He was no doubt inspired by Banjo and Case-on-Case clocks that he had seen, but, by redesigning the layout of the movement, he was able to achieve his aim. He brought the pendulum to the front of the clock just behind the dial, but the motion-work which provides the 1:12 motion of the hands he put between the plates. In a wooden movement these wheels take up quite a lot of room. The movement was against the back of the case as on Willard's patent clock, but the weights hung beside it instead of

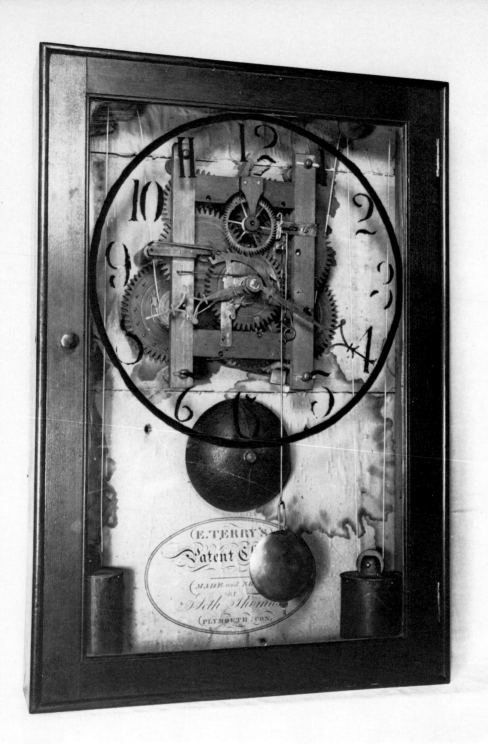

Eli Terry's first shelf clock, made by Seth Thomas, *c.* 1816, with the figures painted on the reverse of the glass. The painted spandrels are now missing, and the pendulum is off-centre. This model was not long in production.

under it, and the cords were carried over pulleys in the top of the case so that the whole height of the latter was available for the weights to fall through. Terry's earliest cases were rectangular and had plain glass doors rendering the movement visible, while the figures were painted on the inside of the glass. A label was stuck into the back of the case giving Terry's name and place of business. Striking was controlled by the rack-and-snail method, unlike the previous Terry clocks that had used count-wheels, and the movement was built up with wooden straps instead of having the solid plates of the earlier clocks. An early experimental model of a weight-driven shelf-clock by Terry is in existence, but it still has the long-case type of arched dial and no striking-work. Terry's new clock dispensed with a dial altogether. It was a magnificent achievement, but it could not be called decorative. The new clock was in production about 1814, Terry having bought another mill and converted it.

It must have been fascinating to the original owners of these Terry clocks to watch the pendulum swinging and see the action of the escapement which was located on the front of the movement. The scapewheel was of brass, as had been the case with the earlier Terry clocks, but otherwise the amount of metal was minimal, and only the metal parts of the clock needed lubrication.

The next development made by Terry was to provide a more ornate case for his shelf-clock movement, and several different models were designed. Some had the entire escapement in front of the dial, while others exposed only the scapewheel. Then the escapement went inside, and sometimes a seconds-hand was fitted. This was facilitated by the use of a half-seconds pendulum.

The new case for these clocks was known as 'the Pillar and Scroll'. The scroll at the top was reminiscent of those often seen on the long-case clocks, and the case was veneered and given a quality finish. The door extended over the whole front of the case and was divided into an upper portion with plain glass to expose the dial and a lower portion containing a glass tablet with a coloured painting to hide the pendulum, although it was usual to leave a tiny portion of the glass clear to allow the bob to be seen. This had been a feature of the Willard Banjo clocks. Some of the Terry designs had the pendulum off-centre, and so the plain portion of the glass had to be off-centre too. The Pillar-and-Scroll case remained fairly consistent in design, but Terry was always revising the design of the movement and went from the strap type to solid plates and changed from rack striking to

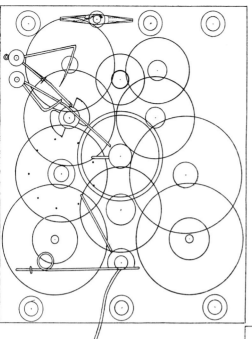

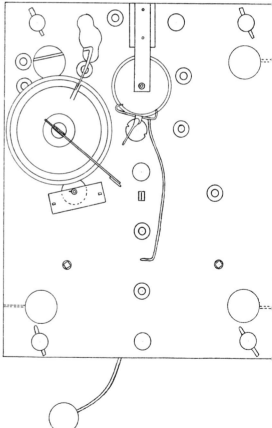

Opposite: The same clock movement
with, right and below right, a side-
view of the going-train and motion-
work, and, far right, a side-view of
the striking-train.

Above: A Terry-type shelf-clock
movement: its layout of trains. Right:
The same – the front plate with the
count-wheel and escapement.

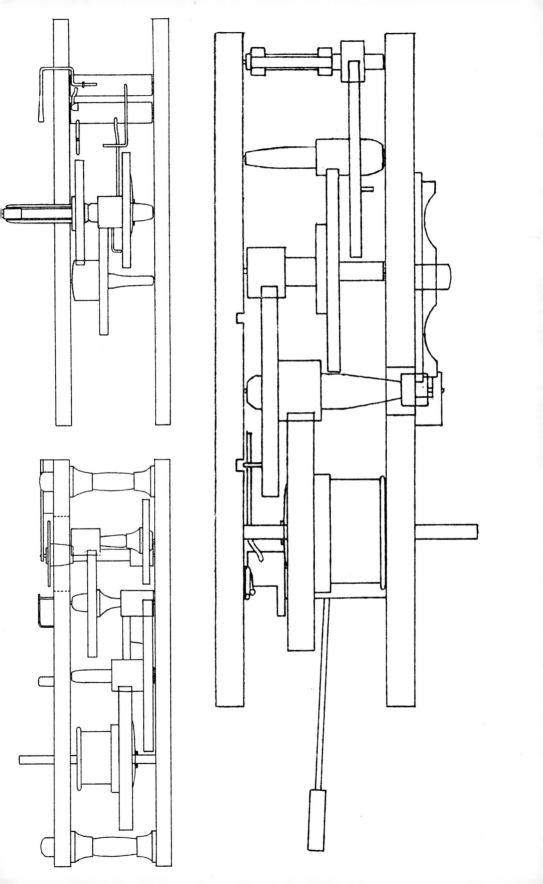

count-wheel, possibly because of the difficulty in making a wooden rack small enough that would stand up to the work.

Terry movements of the plate type as used in the original hang-up clocks are quite difficult to assemble, hence his use of the strap-type movement in his early shelf clocks. The later shelf clocks with the solid-plate movements are even more difficult to assemble owing to the extra arbors in the train, so there must have been a good reason for discarding the strap type of frame. Possibly it was not rigid enough.

Terry obtained a patent for his shelf clock in 1816 and two years later a further patent for the improved model. In 1818 Seth Thomas was granted a licence to make the Terry clock at a royalty of 50 cents per clock, which was later changed to a down payment of $1,000. The new shelf clock was undermining the market for the old type of movement which Seth Thomas had continued to make, and circumstances forced him to change his product.

During the early 1820s the Terry Pillar-and-Scroll design reigned supreme, and many people were making it, mostly without licence. Clocks produced in Connecticut were being sold in all the United States and Canada, mostly by travelling salesmen who specialized in this form of merchandise. About 1825, however, a new design of case was introduced, called 'the Bronze Looking-Glass' clock, which was taller than the Pillar and Scroll but simpler and therefore cost less to make. The new design became so popular that it drove the Pillar and Scroll off the market. The painted tablet was replaced by a looking-glass, and the 'Bronze' in the title referred to the bronze paint used in the decoration of the case. The case was surmounted by a scroll that was much less graceful than that on the Pillar-and-Scroll type, and the dial was somewhat smaller.

As the 1820s passed into the 1830s, the long-case clock virtually disappeared from the market. In Britain the design was to last some fifty years more, but in America the Connecticut factory-made shelf clock had carried all before it. During the 1830s the so called 'Empire' style case was popular. It was tall, like the Bronze Looking-Glass case, but the finish was of higher quality than the latter, and the case was divided into two parts by a moulding in the centre. Heavy paw feet supported it.

The Bronze Looking-Glass clock was usually fitted with a wooden movement, but about 1830 Joseph Ives produced a brass eight-day movement made from rolled brass which had been prepared for other

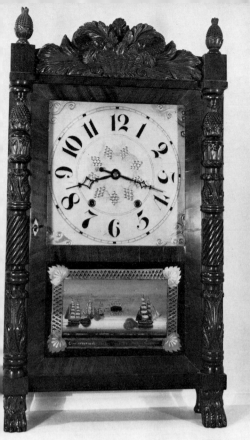 

Left: A carved-column shelf clock with carved splat and pineapple finials, wooden dial and wooden thirty-hour movement, *c.* 1830. The tablet shows "*Constitution*'s escape from the British squadron". Right: An eight-day brass-movement clock from the Forestville Manufacturing Company 1835–9. Note the solid scapewheel and count-wheel spaced for 2×12 hours.

industries. Some of the Bronze Looking-Glass type have been seen with Ives movements, but these movements were for eight-day clocks. All thirty-hour clocks, whether of the long-case or shelf type, were fitted with wooden movements at this period if they came from factories. It is worthy of note that many of the clocks made in Lancaster County, Pennsylvania, which were of the long-case type and made by individual craftsmen, had been fitted with thirty-hour movements, but these were of brass and were even an improvement on the typical thirty-hour long-case movement then being made in Britain. The Pennsylvania clocks always had rack-striking, and the ratchet work for winding was of a much better design than the British clocks possessed.

The 1830s saw the development of railroads, steamboats and canals, which meant that the business of selling wooden clocks could extend over a wider area. By 1835, however, the Southern States were not encouraging Yankee peddlers and put prohibitive taxes on the clocks. Some of the Connecticut manufacturers got over this problem by sending cases of parts to the South and opening assembly-plants where clocks could be assembled and sold as being made in that state. This, however, lasted only a year or two, for the financial situation of the country virtually terminated all business, and many clock firms were forced to end their activities.

The mid-1830s marked a turning-point in the history of the American clock. By this time the old type of clock made by hand was well on the way out, and the Connecticut factories had everything their own way. The shortage of money led to general stagnation in trade, and clocks are one of the first commodities to be hit by a depression. For just thirty years the wooden-movement clock had proved that even poorer homes can be provided with a clock when production is in bulk. The shortage of metal greatly helped to popularize the wooden clock, and the increasing number of immigrants provided the necessary customers. While some of the eighteenth-century clocks had been very close to their British prototypes, there were already signs of a break from tradition when a clockmaker lived in an isolated place and supplies of metal were short. The Case-on-Case types and the Banjo showed some suggestions of French influence, and the wooden hang-up clocks that formed the subject of Terry's first mass-production project, although based on the British eight-day long-case movement, showed Continental influence in the use of wood as material. The wooden clock is particularly associated with the Black Forest of Germany, but the American movements differed from the Black Forest product in that the wheels were held between two plates instead of in a birdcage frame, and the pinions were solid instead of being the lantern-pinions incorporating wire that were used in Germany. The teeth of the wheels leaned forward a little in the American clocks to facilitate meshing with the solid pinions, while Black Forest teeth are usually upright.

The Pennsylvania long-case clocks of the thirty-hour type were broadly built to conform to the British model and had plate frames, but many of the German clockmakers in the area used lantern-pinions in their clocks and suspended the pendulum from cord instead of a spring. These clocks were cheaper than those of the British pattern, and the customer would specify his requirements.

Pillar and Scroll Shelf clock.
Eli and Samuel Terry, 1825-29

The same clock
showing the movement

Long Case, *c.* 1820. Note the inlay is more elaborate than on a typical British clock of this period

COLLECTORS' ITEMS

The types of clock that we have been considering so far have formed collectors' items for a long time, and they are highly prized in the country of their origin. They are not widely known outside America as they were never items of export, and in the past clock-collectors have tended very much to specialize in the products of their own country and ignore others. Prices are naturally very high, and the Banjo type in particular is in great demand, hence a great deal of faking has been done to clocks of this type and such things have occurred as several broken clocks of the type being combined to make one good one and accessories and tablets of a wrong period being fitted to a clock that lacked them. Those signed 'S. Willard' are naturally the most sought-after and therefore the most obvious ones to suffer at the hands of a faker. Clocks without a signature could also be easily provided with one.

The long-case or 'tall' clock, as it is known in America, is also extremely popular as a collector's item and has suffered in the same way as the Banjo. Wooden movements will have suffered through damp and central heating but are capable of repair, and with the interest in horology that has developed in the last few years has come a number of people both amateur and professional who are capable of restoring such movements. Not only restoration has been undertaken but also the construction of new movements of the type, as various firms have produced and published drawings showing how the work should be done.

Hands can often get changed and are not reliable for dating a clock. Sometimes one hand will be replaced and the design will clash with that of the other one. The design of hands on long-case clocks of the eighteenth-century type were very similar to those in use in Britain, and in fact many of them would have been obtained from Britain by American clockmakers either finished or in the rough state for finishing. There is a tendency for hands on American long-case clocks to be slightly more decorated than those in Britain, and this may indicate that they were locally made.

Hands on the smaller clocks such as the Case on Case and the Banjo are plainer than those on the long-case clocks. Some of the Terry shelf clocks had hands of the same length but with the hour-hand made broader to contrast with the minute-hand. On these clocks the minute-marks are inside the hour-marks, suggesting early

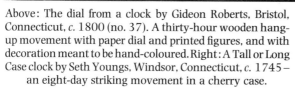

Above: The dial from a clock by Gideon Roberts, Bristol, Connecticut, *c.* 1800 (no. 37). A thirty-hour wooden hang-up movement with paper dial and printed figures, and with decoration meant to be hand-coloured. Right: A Tall or Long Case clock by Seth Youngs, Windsor, Connecticut, *c.* 1745 – an eight-day striking movement in a cherry case.

dials in South Germany and Austria. Pewter hands are also seen on early shelf clocks, but later ones were of iron. Some country makers used wooden hands, but generally speaking they were of iron.

The smaller clocks, such as the Case-on-Case type and the few bracket spring-driven clocks of the British type that were made in the USA, are also out of range of the general collector of today. The shelf clocks with wooden movements were made in thousands, and, though there has been a large number of casualties among them, sufficient remain for them to be more widely spread than the other types of clock. They are, however, rapidly entering the top price-bracket, and as all of them are still virtually in their country of origin, the collector from elsewhere will not stand much chance of acquiring one.

The collector of today who is interested in American clocks must therefore turn his attention to the many examples from factories that poured across the Atlantic after 1842. They necessarily had metal movements as the wooden movements would not stand up to a long sea-voyage, and right from the start they were intended for the lower-price market. The export venture was successful, and the clocks came over in hundreds of thousands for nearly sixty years. Developments in technology led to modifications in design, and the constant variations that one meets add to the interest of collecting this type of clock. A few years ago these clocks were gaily thrown away as no one was interested in them, but as higher prices and diminishing supplies put the more expensive British or Continental clocks out of the buyers' range, attention was diverted to the humbler products from the American factories. One is comparatively secure in this market as it has never been worthwhile to do any alteration or faking to these clocks, and even the higher prices paid for them today do not encourage this, as the cost of the work would absorb too much of the cost price of the clocks. There is the additional fact that, since these clocks have become popular, a new public has emerged that knows far more about the construction of clocks than collectors did in the past. The collector of yesterday worried most about the case, but nowadays there are many amateurs who can detect not only mechanical faults in movements but also pieces of the wrong design that have been added.

In subsequent chapters we will turn our attention to the numerous types of clock that were produced by American factories. A complete list of all the types has not been made and probably never will be, because something new is constantly turning up, and even the names of some of the firms on their labels have not been seen before. The collector of American factory clocks has been greatly helped in recent years by the re-publication of many of the old catalogues which help in the identification of various models and also show the dates when such a clock was popular. A new aspect of the subject has been raised in recent years by collectors who take an interest in the clocks produced in the Black Forest which were based on American models, and it is an interesting exercise to decide whether a clock that is encountered is of German or American origin. By the beginning of the twentieth century the Black Forest had recovered its place in the British market, and some of the post-1900 American catalogues contain clocks which are rarely if ever seen in Britain. The collecting of American clocks still offers a great deal of scope for today's collector, and even the beginner will find that there is plenty of research still to do.

An OG with alarm mechanism by Chauncey Jerome, Bristol, Connecticut, 1840–45.

2   The OG

The OG is far and away the most important clock that America has produced. The name was derived from the ogive, which was the shape of the moulding that formed the front of the case surrounding the door which gave access to the dial and movement. Some cases were eventually modified to have the beading that covered the outer edge of the moulding made convex and the pieces of wood that formed the door made concave. These clocks were called 'Double OG' or 'OOG'. For decorative purposes the grain of the veneer on the OG moulding went across instead of parallel to the length, and when there was a great contrast between light and dark portions of the grain, this was known as 'Tiger'.

The OG pioneered the use of a brass movement in a one-day clock and thereby opened the door to the export market. The old wooden clocks were sensitive to journeys over water, and while they could tolerate a day or two on a canal barge, the Atlantic crossing was too long. The wooden-movement clocks were all absorbed by the home market, particularly by the Southern states, and until the metal movement allowed production in greater quantity than ever before, an export market was not possible. The financial crisis of 1837 was the beginning of a chain of events that led to the establishment of overseas trade owing to the stagnation at home, and once exporting was established, it continued to increase until the end of the century. The business in wooden movements was virtually over by about 1844. Not only were the new metal movements easier to make and more reliable, but the material for the wooden movements was becoming more difficult to get. Thirty-odd years of production by numerous firms had consumed the supplies of suitable woods, and unless the materials are of the finest quality, a wooden movement is useless. Moreover, the OG began the practice of making a movement smaller, which, when mainsprings could be produced economically in America, led to clocks themselves being smaller also.

JEROME'S OG

Chauncey Jerome was one of the largest producers of clocks in the USA and therefore was hit very hard by the depression. He tells the story of a trip to Richmond, Virginia, to try to set his affairs in order, and of how he was sitting looking at a wooden-movement clock and wondering how to re-establish his business when the idea came to him of a one-day shelf clock with a brass movement.

Shelf clocks with brass movements were already known, but they always ran for eight days. There were also wooden movements which ran for eight days, but the extra arbors required in the train greatly increased the friction, and therefore much heavier weights were needed which involved more stress on the parts. These clocks are therefore rare. Traditionally the wooden-movement clock ran for one day only, and all shelf clocks which ran for one day had wooden movements.

As we have seen, the nature of wood means that the number of wheels employed in the train has to be increased because the number of teeth that can be cut on each wheel is strictly limited. A clock with brass wheels can have fewer of them as each wheel can be provided with many teeth. A wooden wheel has to be cut from selected timber, planed and turned true and the teeth cut with a circular saw, each tooth involving two cuts. The supply of rolled brass in Connecticut provided sheets that could have circular blanks stamped out of them which could be put together in piles and have the teeth cut in one operation for each space by employing a rotary cutter. The plates of the clock could also be stamped, and by leaving openings in them, assembly was facilitated. The old wooden movements, in spite of the size of the parts, were very difficult to assemble and clumsy to handle. A brass movement could be smaller, and in addition it was not so sensitive to fire hazard or to the effects of a moist atmosphere.

As far as the case was concerned, existing designs could be used, but it would obviously be cheaper to omit all the carving and stencilling added at the time and rely on the finish of the wood to provide the decorative effect. Cases could be made of pine and veneered with mahogany, and the design eventually adopted for the new brass-movement clock was the OG. The case was rectangular, about 26 × 15 inches (66 × 38 centimetres). The door had the usual plain glass over the dial and a coloured tablet at the bottom, and as the door was recessed as a result of the OG moulding, the handle did not project above the surface, thereby facilitating packing. (This feature has also been of use to American collectors of the type who collect them in large quantities and have them stacked up in the garage like cordwood.) The earliest dials were of wood, as on the wooden-movement clocks, and there were already facilities for the supply of weights.

The idea became more exciting as each detail was considered. On his return to Connecticut, Jerome got his brother, Noble Jerome, to design the movement, and this was patented, No. 1,200 of 27th June 1839. The prototype was rough with solid wheels, but the design of the movement scarcely changed through the years during which these clocks were made.

Two important features of the movement were the ridge stamped in the rim of the wheels to give extra strength and the method of strike-control. Brass movements belonging to eight-day clocks were at this time usually provided with the rack-and-snail striking-mechanism, but Noble Jerome reverted to the count-wheel because of its cheapness.

Instead of the count-wheel having a continuous drive from a pinion on the main arbor engaging with a separate toothed wheel concentric with the count-wheel proper, the outer edge of the count-wheel had seventy-eight saw-shaped teeth with slots between at appropriate intervals for controlling the number of blows. The count-wheel was mounted on the frame concentric with the main arbor and was held by a friction-spring. The second arbor of the train, which made one revolution per blow struck, was provided with a pin that advanced the count-wheel one tooth every time the arbor revolved. The count-wheel then remained stationary, held by the friction-spring, until the second arbor revolved once more and advanced the next tooth. The second arbor carried a cam with a slot in it that also revolved once per blow, and a wire lifting-piece had one arm that rode on the cam and one with a flattened end that touched the count-wheel between the teeth at each blow. When the slot in the cam came round, the lifting-piece made its dip, but normally when the lifting-piece was riding on the edge of the cam, the count-wheel arm was raised clear of the saw-edged teeth. As striking progressed, the count-wheel would eventually present a deep slot to the lifting-piece, which would then dip further and lock the train by means of the other arm catching the edge of the slot in the cam. The use of a cam rather than a hoop-wheel was reminiscent of Continental clockmaking rather than British.

Features of the Terry movement that were retained were the placing of the escapement on the front plate and placing the motion-work between the plates, together with mounting the pallets on a fixed pin instead of a movable arbor. The pendulum was still made from a wire with the end beaten out to form a suspension-spring and held in a brass stud on the front plate of the movement. The lines for the weights were carried to pulleys in the top of the case, but that on the striking side had a smaller pulley in the partition as well, to keep the line well clear of the fly.

The first OGs were sold by C. and N. Jerome, Bristol, Connecticut. The next type seen was inscribed 'Jeromes & Co', and in this the traditional design was established with the wheels being crossed out and the paper of instructions pasted in the back of the case. The earliest dials were of wood with brass collets round the winding-holes, but soon dials were being made from sheet zinc. The wood dial was virtually finished by 1850, and the custom of writing the manufacturer's name on the dial did not last long either. The earliest dials had crude paintings of flowers in the corners; after the zinc dial was well established, these became simple monochrome designs and were later discontinued.

In 1839 the Jerome brothers joined with William L. Gilbert and Zelotes Grant to form a firm for producing the new type of clock, and in a year it had become very successful. In 1840 Chauncey bought out the other three partners at a sum considerably more than their original investment.

The story is usually told that he was the pioneer of export to Britain, but this is also claimed for the firm of Sperry & Shaw of New York. In view of the fact that they were located in New York and not Connecticut, it is possible that they were dealers, although they were probably handling Jerome clocks anyway. In 1841 a consignment sent to Britain was seized by the Customs on the grounds that they were undervalued at $1.50 with twenty per cent duty. Mr Sperry had travelled with the consignment and satisfied the authorities that the price was genuine, and on the cargo's release he managed to sell them at £4–5 each, that is about $20.

Jerome's own version of the story is that he sent out a consignment in 1842, being the pioneer, and the clocks were seized by the Customs who paid him ten per cent above invoice prices. He then sent another which was dealt with in the same way, but when the third arrived, the Customs decided to let them through.

Whichever version of the story is correct, there can be no doubt that there was a rich market in Britain, and the number of clocks from America increased yearly. As time went on, new styles of clock made their appearance, but the OG remained a firm favourite to the end of the century. It was a good timekeeper; there were no springs to break; it ran with the minimum of maintenance and took up comparatively little room. It was more sophisticated than the Black Forest wall clock with exposed weights and pendulum and gradually drove the latter off the market. Not only in Britain but also in Europe the effect of the new style of clock was felt. Hamburg began to receive consignments as well as Liverpool.

OG VARIATIONS

The eight-day weight-driven shelf clock with brass movement had been well known in the USA before 1840, and, along with the production of thirty-hour clocks by improved methods, the eight-day movement was also re-designed. While cases prior to 1840 were more highly decorated with carving or stencilling, the eight-day clock began to be made in increasing numbers in the plain OG case, usually measuring 32×17 inches ($81\frac{1}{2} \times 42\frac{1}{2}$ centimetres). From the 1840s to the 1880s the eight-day clocks were also made with cases having heavy half-columns beside the door, and sometimes a separate base with its own separate door and tablet. The affinity between these clocks and the OG was simply in the brass movement which was produced by more efficient methods, but a new design of case based on the thirty-hour OG also appeared having the columns, usually with gilt capitals, and while these clocks had the normal thirty-hour OG movement, they do not qualify for the title of OG because the special moulding is missing.

Between 1849 and 1859 the firm of Birge Peck & Co supplied eight-day weight-driven clocks, some with the conventional column-type cases but others in the older 'three-decker' style, where the case had three separate doors or two doors and a fixed centre tablet. These cases usually included some carving, and as the firm used the old type of movement with the plates built up of brass strips riveted together rather than stamped from solid sheet brass, the clocks appear older than they actually are.

The eight-day movements made prior to 1840 and also later, sometimes employed a count-wheel provided with two sets of twelve hour-divisions, introduced by Joseph Ives, which moved with the great wheel, but after the establishment of the Noble Jerome movement, the eight-day movements were also produced with the count-wheel that moved intermittently.

Left: The Brewster single-pin strike movement. The pin for operating the hammer is visible at the right-hand side of the cam. Right: An eight-day column clock by Birge & Fuller, 1844–8. The label contains an illustration of an early locomotive.

Jerome's initial success encouraged other manufacturers to enter the field, just as Terry's production had thirty years previously. Seth Thomas tried to remain in the wooden clock business, but he eventually started making metal-movement OGs, and his clocks are the most solid of any so far noted. Some of the later Jeromes leave something to be desired: the dies got blunt, and the wheels were stamped with ragged edges to the crossings, so that more than one Jerome movement has had its parts crack in course of time, showing stresses on the metal.

Many different papers are seen in the backs of OG cases, but in many instances these are papers of dealers only and not of manufacturers. The equipment for making movements was expensive, and it was easier to acquire them from specialist firms and make the cases or buy in the latter from other specialist firms.

Chauncey Jerome's brother Noble and Zelotes Grant formed a

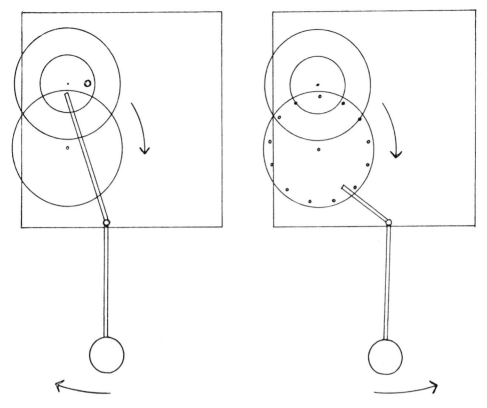

The difference between the Brewster single-pin strike and the normal method of striking as used in an OG. The arrows show the direction in which the hammer is raised.

company (Jerome Grant & Co) for making movements and supplied Chauncey with a number in the early 1840s. While taking supplies from this firm, Chauncey continued to run his own movement shop, supervised by his nephew Hiram Camp. In 1845 Chauncey's factory in Bristol was burned down, and he then moved his operations to New Haven. OG clocks marked 'Chauncey Jerome, Bristol' are rare in Britain, but they can be dated exactly from 1840–45. The ones made in New Haven are much commoner.

Many of the earlier movements are very much alike, and without the firm name stamped on them, it is difficult to give their origin. Variations in the original design are rare, the most important being those with the Davis striking-mechanism and those with the Brewster single-pin strike. The Davis striking-mechanism is very complicated, being a combination of count-wheel and rack, and is extremely rare. The Brewster mechanism is, however, quite simple, and it is a mystery why the design was not adopted by more manufacturers.

A normal OG movement has thirteen pins in the rim of the great wheel which raise the hammer. The next arbor of the train carries the cam that controls the locking and the pin for moving the count-wheel one tooth every time it revolves. The Brewster system omits the thirteen pins on the great wheel, substitutes a single pin on the cam for moving the hammer and has it in such a position that the hammer-tail falls immediately prior to locking. This has the advantage of saving labour in drilling the wheel-rim and inserting the pins, and also needs no adjustment of the striking-train to arrange locking immediately after the hammer has fallen. When making movements in thousands, this could have a marked effect on production-costs. On the Brewster movement a ridge is stamped not only into the wheels for strengthening purposes but also in the plates themselves. A clock with this movement can be easily distinguished without removing the dial by noting that the hammer moves to the left on being raised and to the right when striking the gong, just the reverse of the normal OG movement. Brewster movements have so far been seen marked 'Brewster & Ingrahams' (1844–52), 'E. C. Brewster & Son' (1855) and 'E. C. Brewster & Co' (1840–43). The design was probably due to Charles Kirk, movement-shop foreman to Brewster, or his successor, Anson Atwood.

Movements by the Seth Thomas organization are generally very similar to Jerome's and usually have the firm's name stamped on them. Eight-day movements by this firm are usually in the shape of a lyre. Movements by the Waterbury Clock Company do not usually have the stiffening rims stamped into the wheels. The New Haven Clock Company often stamped its monogram into the plate near the winding-square for the going-train, while the labels often bear the name 'Jerome & Co'. The New Haven Clock Company took over the Jerome business after Chauncey went bankrupt in 1855 and continued to use the name Jerome on account of the goodwill.

The coloured tablets on the doors can give a clue to dating. The earliest nearly always showed a scene or building such as 'The Merchants' Exchange at Philadelphia' or some similar subject. Brewster & Ingrahams used etched glass on some occasions, as on their other models. Later designs consisted of a plain background with flowers or fruit as the centrepiece. Seth Thomas often surrounded the central design with an oval, while Waterbury favoured a circular surround. Late New Haven tablets usually have a central scene with black surround decorated by gilt lines. The use of a mirror for a tablet is generally a sign of an early clock, as is also a tablet with etched glass.

One early design of Jerome hands was very simple with a circular piece of metal left on each side of a straight slender hand to render the end more easily visible. Many firms, including Jerome's, used the type of hand with a ring near the end, especially Seth Thomas's. Brewster & Ingrahams used a plain minute-hand with a very small spade on the hour-hand. The Seth Thomas idea of advertising the firm by making the end of the minute hand an 'S' with that of the hour hand a 'T' seems to have been used on their smaller models only. The Maltese Cross design for hands is found on clocks after about 1860.

The OG is far and away the type of American clock most frequently met with in Britain, accounting for some forty per cent of the total. The rapidity with which the clocks sold encouraged other manufacturers to enter the business, and even the conservative Seth Thomas gave up making wooden movements for brass ones. As in the case of the Terry shelf clock, there was the awkward question of the patent, and steps were taken to avoid paying royalties if possible.

An interesting example has been noted which suggests that it may have been made with a view to avoiding the problems connected with patent rights. It is probably quite early, as the dial is of wood and decorated with coloured paintings in the corners, while the winding-holes are protected by heavy brass rings. The clock is slightly smaller than usual, measuring $25\frac{1}{4} \times 14\frac{3}{4}$ inches ($64 \times 37\frac{1}{2}$ centimetres), and the OG moulding has a sharper curve. The hinges of the doors are formed from brass wires, and the plain oval (left on the tablet so that the pendulum-bob can be seen) actually comes well above the bob so that the plain portion of the glass is meaningless. This seems to indicate that tablets were sold to fit the normal size of clock, and if that size were departed from, situations such as this arose.

The movement differs from the conventional type by having the count-wheel fitted on the inside of the back plate, hence the pins in the rim of the great wheel for lifting the hammer point forwards instead of backwards. The count-wheel driving-pin is one of the wires of the pinion on the second arbor which protrudes through its shroud, and it points towards the back plate. The wire, which hangs down for allowing the striking-train to be released if it gets out of step with the hands, is supported by the wire that rides on the cam instead of the wire that dips into the slots of the count-wheel. As the latter is at the rear of the movement, it would be more awkward to raise the wire if it were very near the back of the case. The strike-release wire is compelled to pass through a hole in the seatboard.

The solid brass wheel on the centre arbor that is driven by the main wheel is left solid instead of having a number of circular holes drilled in it as on most movements. The nuts for holding the movement on to the seatboard are square instead of being round as on most clocks.

The most unusual thing about the clock is its paper. This is complete and contains the usual instructions for setting the clock running and regulating it etc, but it bears no maker's name or that of a vendor or even a printer. Where the gong-base is fixed is a representation of a carved Empire-style clock of the 1830–40 period which is quite often seen on various clock-papers, but when the gong base is in position, the drawing is invisible.

CLOCK-PAPERS AND OTHER MEANS OF DATING

The dating of a given example of an OG is something that can be learned only by experience. Reference-books can give the dates that the various firms were in operation, and other features such as the design of the dial, tablet etc can give clues to narrow-down the date of production. Early Jerome cases were rebated at the corners instead of being mitred as on later clocks, and the quality of the finish is much higher.

The early features such as a wooden dial have already been dealt with, but late features are the use of hexagonal nuts to secure the movement to the seatboard, rounded corners to the plates, plates excessively bright, showing that they have been 'treated' in some way, and conventional 'spade' hands. An embossed pendulum-bob is a late feature, and if this is found on a clock which has features that are otherwise considered early, it is a replacement. Sometimes bobs are marked 'HPF'. This stands for 'Henri Picard et Frère', a firm of material dealers established in the 1870s and which is still in existence. These bobs, having been made in Britain, would be replacements. The iron base for the gong was covered with pressed brass in many cases, the earlier ones being plain and the later ones decorated, particularly those used by William Gilbert. By the end of the nineteenth century the covers had been discontinued as they were not functional and cost money.

In 1874 Waterbury introduced a new method of releasing the striking which allowed the hands to be turned backwards. Instead of having an L-shaped piece of wire fixed in the centre arbor for the purpose of raising the lifting-piece, this was done by a small triangular piece of brass. If the hands were turned back, the oblique edge of the brass piece just pushed the lifting-piece aside and did not affect the striking-train. If the hands were turned back on the old type of strike-release, the L-shaped piece of wire would catch in the loop of the lifting-piece and jam. If a Waterbury clock is seen with the new device and yet carries a paper saying that the hands must not be turned back, a date of about 1874 can be inferred. Some Waterbury clocks of this period carry the old paper and in addition have a new one pasted on the back of the case outside saying that the hands can be turned back.

The early papers always bore the title 'Brass Clocks' to draw attention to their novelty. The words 'Improved' or 'Extra Bushed' are also found, the extra bushing being on the main arbors that feel the direct pull of the weights and therefore need extra bearing-surface.

The paper was well-known in the wooden clocks, but in the OG it reached its fullest development. The wording is very similar whoever may have produced the clock, but detailed instructions are given for setting up the clock and applying oil at various points, and these places are the same as on the old wooden clocks, i.e. those parts of the movement which were made of metal in the older type. The oiling of the escapement was facilitated by the large opening in the centre of the dial. In the wooden clocks, only those places where metal worked against metal were oiled. The iron pivots working in wooden holes were left dry.

Some clocks are found where the instructions mention that the clock can be set up without removing the hands and dial, and yet the dial has only a small hole in the centre, which would preclude any oil being applied to the escapement. Such dials are in the minority, and one can only conclude that they were provided for a small number of customers who preferred not to see the movement through the dial, and it was not worth the trouble to have special labels printed for these clocks.

Regulation by raising or lowering the bob was dealt with, and the setting of the striking if it got out of step with the time shown by the hands. A rather curious point is that many papers give the instruction to put the light weight on the strike side of the clock when little difference can be detected between the two weights.

If a clock is to be accepted as a collector's item, the paper must be in good condition. Many clocks have had their papers ripped out, and there is no clue to the maker if the movement is not stamped. Some papers are nearly all gone, but sometimes it is possible to reconstruct the name from the portions that remain.

When clocks became spring-driven and therefore smaller, the paper was necessarily reduced in size, and for this reason the clock-paper is at its largest and most complete in the OG. A view of the maker's factory would impress the customer, and often horses and carts or even trains were shown carrying away the products. The paper should always be well looked after, and it should be remembered that it was very thin to start off with and has become dry and brittle during the century or so of its existence.

Some movements, including Jerome's, are so made that they can take alarm work, and the holes for the extra pivots are often found although no mechanism is fitted. It was easier in the factory to make all plates alike and fit the alarm-mechanism only to the number of clocks that was suggested by recent sales figures. Most catalogues illustrate models that can carry alarm-work, and the charge is usually something like 50 cents extra. The alarm was released by means of a brass disc carrying a cam with a slot that rode on the hour-wheel pipe. The hammer-tail bore on the cam, and when the slot came round, the alarm-work could operate as the hammer was then free to move. The time for sounding the alarm was controlled by turning the disc until the hour desired came below the hour-hand, or sometimes to a position opposite the hour-hand, in which case the latter had a short rearward extension for more exact indication. This simple idea was a legacy from the older wooden-movement clocks.

Seth Thomas OGs began to be made about 1844. The business became a company in 1853, and in 1869 the name of the place where the factory was situated was changed from Plymouth Hollow to Thomaston in honour of the founder of the firm. Some of the labels were printed by Elihu Geer, and as this printer changed his address fairly frequently, it gives a clue to the dating of the clocks. It should not be forgotten that a batch of labels printed by the firm were not

Eight-day Column clock by Birge Peck and Co. Bristol, Conn., 1849-59. The strap movement used by this firm suggests that the clocks are older than they really are

(top left) OG by Seth Thomas

(top right) Brewster and Ingrahams
eight-day OG with
continental-style tablet

(left) Thirty-hour Column clock
by Seth Thomas

necessarily used on clocks until possibly a year later, as it was cheaper to print in quantity and lay in a good stock. Geer was located in State Street, Hartford, and his address changed as follows: 1839–44 26½; 1845–6 26; 1847–9 No 1; 1850–5 No 10; 1856–64 No 16, and after 1865 No 18. By 1863 Francis & Loutrel of New York City were doing printing for Seth Thomas.

Some of the catalogues reprinted by the American Clock and Watch Museum (which supplied the information on the printer noted above) contain dates when a certain model was discontinued. Many of the older models were in the Seth Thomas catalogues until 1913, but this does not imply that they were still being made. The year in which various models disappear shows the year in which the remainder of the stock had been sold out.

A very charming variation of the OG is the miniature. This is a scaled-down version of the standard size but generally employs a spring-driven movement as the distance through which the weights can fall is limited. As spring clocks, they belong to the period after 1850, the earliest reference to them in a catalogue being that for Seth Thomas in 1863. The miniatures are not very common, but both thirty-hour and eight-day versions have been seen.

Among the last OGs to be made were those of the New Haven Clock Company. They can be detected by their labels, which are printed in the Art Nouveau style and include a view of a very large factory.

Most OG movements have a small hole near the second arbor of the striking-train which apparently has no function. This hole would be used for locating the jig when the plate was made. Door-handles can vary from a proper casting to a piece of wire split down the middle and bent into two loops.

As far as is known, the American OG remained fairly consistent to the original design throughout the period during which it was made. Occasionally an example is seen where the door is gilt or some other difference in decoration is observed, but it should be apparent from inspection whether these differences are original. Replacement dials used to be sold by material-dealers, and they had a hole only in the centre, leaving the repairer to drill the holes for the winding-squares where necessary. The centre hole was just large enough to admit the hour-hand pipe and did not expose the escapement. These dials also give themselves away by having figures which are shorter than the originals. It was a feature of the OG dial to have very long slender figures with prominent serifs.

Left: A miniature OG with spring-driven movement by Jerome & Co, 18 inches high.
Right: A miniature wall clock approximating to the OG design by Seth Thomas.

OGs are sometimes seen with a Holloway & Co label. The firm's trademark consisting of a crown and 'H & Co' was usually embossed on the back of the case. These clocks used American movements but were probably cased in London (see Chapter 7), and while the firm made the conventional OG type, they also supplied a spring-driven variety. Their own paper was pasted into the back, usually printed on a brick-coloured ground. The tablets are usually more reminiscent of Continental clocks such as those supplied by Junghans, and the cases also show a similarity to the Junghans product.

PRESERVING THE OG

Until recently the OG has not been a collector's item, and therefore few people have bothered to restore them or even repair them when they ceased to function. The clocks have been consigned to the woodshed or the attic until the interest shown in recent years has brought them out again. The cases are made only of soft wood and are therefore liable to worm. If the rear of the case has been severely attacked, this can result in the paper becoming damaged and can require new wood to be inserted to replace the old. This will have an effect on the smell of the clock. The OG has a very distinctive odour owing to the use of coniferous wood, and this is so well-known that a clock can be spoiled as a collector's piece if it does not possess the familiar odour.

An OG is a clock that will fit into a modern setting as it is usually hung on the wall, and in this age of rooms without mantelpieces this is a distinct advantage. Strangely enough, they were designed as shelf clocks like their wooden-wheeled predecessors, and yet practically every example encountered in Britain has had a hole drilled in the back so that the clock can be hung on the wall. Even if the gongs sound very unmelodious, they can be corrected (see Chapter 8), and only recently, a service has been started to supply replacement-tablets that will do a great deal to improve the appearance of a battered example. The veneer can usually be repolished to shine with its former brilliance, and replacing veneer is not all that difficult. Some people paint the cases white or in a bright colour, but this is definitely wrong! It is also possible to get dials restored. While some Americans collect the clocks in piles, the OG is essentially a clock to be lived with, and it will keep good time and add something to any room in whatever style it is furnished.

3   The Mainspring

The use of the mainspring as motive-power for clocks may date from as early as the beginning of the fifteenth century. The production of a long flexible ribbon of steel that was capable of being wound up and released an infinite number of times without breaking was quite an achievement and would have been a job in the first instance for a sword-maker. Probably several attempts would have had to be made before a spring that was satisfactory could be produced. In those days the production of steel was a difficult and laborious process, and it was not until the nineteenth century that most of the difficulties were overcome. After the ribbon had been forged, it had to be smoothed on a long table and then hardened and tempered. A high polish was necessary to reduce friction as the coils rubbed over each other. The spring was then coiled into its container, known as a barrel.

By the sixteenth century the spring was firmly established in spite of the difficulties of manufacture, and during the two following centuries the production of spring clocks went on increasing. The spring was particularly popular in France, and American clock-makers would import their springs from that country as well as from Switzerland. It was, of course, only in rare instances that springs were required in America in the eighteenth and early nineteenth centuries. British clockmakers insisted on a fusee where spring clocks were concerned, in order to even up the power supplied to the train, but French makers abandoned it early, and most French clocks were made with the springs driving the wheels directly.

A spring to be used with a fusee has to be stiffer and not so long as one that drives directly. A few bracket clocks on the British model were made in the USA, but the early use of the spring in that country occurs mostly in shelf-clocks with brass movements having cases resembling the Terry Pillar and Scroll and dating from the early part of the nineteenth century. These clocks were individually made and quite rare.

When a spring is used with a normal type of fusee, as in European clocks, it has to be contained in a barrel. This is a drum usually made of brass, and as the spring unwinds, it causes the barrel to rotate and winds the line on the outer surface as it is pulled off the fusee. The barrel is mounted on an iron or steel arbor which is supported at its ends by the plates of the movement. The ends of the barrel, or 'covers', have a central hole for mounting on the arbor, and the cover is usually thicker at this point to increase the bearing-surface. One cover is fixed and the other removable to allow the spring and the arbor to be inserted. The removable cover is fastened in position by a snap fit, and the covers rotate with the barrel while the arbors remain stationary. The shoulders on the arbor where the covers come have to be well finished and smooth to minimize friction and accurately dimensioned so that there is not too much end-movement, or 'endshake'. If this were excessive, the line might slip from the edge of the barrel.

The barrel arbor has to have one end made square to take the ratchet allowing the spring to be set up with a little tension when the line is all on the barrel and the clock cannot run down any further. The ratchet involves the use of a thick piece of brass, and another piece is required for the click, while the barrel and the arbor also require a certain amount of metal for their making.

The British clockmaker would always test every spring fitted to a clock by means of a testing-rod. Each spring had its own individuality and in theory required a fusee to be specially made for it. With the aid of a testing-rod, the power supplied by the mainspring at all stages of the run could be examined and the fusee adjusted accordingly. This was a time-consuming job. The movement had to be assembled, the mainspring set up, the testing-rod applied, the places noted where the power varied, the clock taken to pieces, the fusee corrected and the clock re-assembled for the whole process to be begun again. There was also the chance that the spring could break after the fusee had been corrected, and this would involve a new spring and the whole process being carried out once more. Add in the cost of labour of finishing the extra parts required, and it will be seen that there was not much incentive to depart from the weight-driven clock on the part of the American clockmaker. Orders for a more elaborate clock would be rare and could be given by only the richest of customers. Hanging over the clockmaker's head was always the problem connected with the shortage of metal. It can be seen that the more expensive market in America would be better catered for by such weight-driven clocks as the Banjo.

MAINSPRING PIONEERS

One of the pioneers of the use of the mainspring in America was Joseph Ives. During the 1820s he was working in New York, having previously been bankrupted in Bristol, Connecticut, and during this period he produced a number of clocks with spring-drive. He was by no means the first American clockmaker to use a mainspring, but his aim was to overcome the difficulties that limited the use of springs and render this form of motive-power more popular. The cases of the clocks that he produced in New York were more slender and graceful than the Terry Pillar-and-Scroll type of which they were the contemporaries, and the movements showed some unusual features. As in the Banjo type, the upper part containing the movement was circular and very little larger than the dial, and the base of the case was rectangular with a glass tablet in the door. The central portion was, however, much smaller. Ives did not use a coiled spring but arranged very strong, short, flat springs in the bottom of the case which drove the movement through pivoted levers arranged to compensate for the difference in power as the spring ran down. The spring consisted of a number of strips of steel firmly fixed in the centre, and as they resembled the compound spring used on a wagon, the term 'Wagon Spring' is now applied to the clocks by collectors. This type of spring showed an economy of metal compared with a normal coiled spring.

The importance of Ives's design lies as much in the compensation for varying torque as in the basic idea. His first clock used springs of a different nature with a kind of fusee compensation, but this was placed in a Pillar-and-Scroll case driving a normal movement with wooden wheels and really achieved very little. It was on the later clocks that could be made smaller that the idea really came into its own. Ives's New York clocks had metal movements, small at first but later enlarged in order to get a better gear-ratio and reduce friction. The gearing in the earlier models left something to be desired in spite of the use of roller-pinions, another of Ives's innovations. Unfortunately Ives did not prosper, and few of these clocks were made. They are, of course, highly prized in America.

A variation of the wagon-spring was to mount a curved spring in the top of the case at the centre with the two ends hanging beside the movement. The ends of the spring were attached by cords to fusees in the movement, and as the clock was wound, the ends of the spring

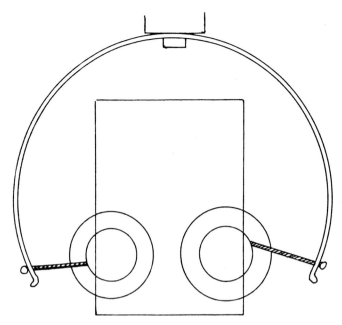

An early method of using a leaf-spring, by Joseph Ives. The ends of the spring are pulled down and towards the movement as the cords are wound onto the fusees.

were drawn in towards the centre. As the clock ran, they would open out and drive the movement by pulling the cords off the fusees.

The most famous application of Ives's idea was on a number of clocks made by Birge & Fuller in the mid-1840s. Ives obtained a patent for a new method of equalizing the power by the intervention of drums driven by chains off the lever-system. The drums in their turn pulled cords which were wound on to the barrels of what was a normal OG movement.

Joseph Shaylor Ives, a nephew of Joseph Ives, invented main-springs made of brass in 1836. The only way to harden brass is by work-hardening, i.e. by rolling, hammering or drawing into wire. Brass springs were used for some years and proved quite satisfactory, except that they fatigue in time. The rolled-brass industry in Connecticut was developing in the 1830s and led the way to Noble Jerome's cheap brass movement, so there was no problem over the supply of raw material for the brass springs. The weight of the springs is considerable. In spite of this, there was a great incentive to use them as the cost per pair was only 50 cents compared with $3 as the cost of a pair of imported steel springs. Joseph Shaylor Ives also obtained a patent for applying springs to a normal Terry-type

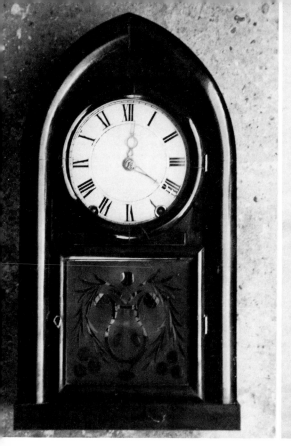

An eight-day Beehive by Brewster & Ingrahams, 1844–52. Left: Wooden dial, ground-glass tablet and brass hands. Right: The movement. Note the design of the gong-base.

movement with wooden wheels and plates, but clocks made on this principle are very rare indeed. The importance of the idea was that the springs drove the main arbors directly without the intervention of fusees.

The use of a normal OG movement had already been made in spring-driven clocks by E. C. Brewster, who housed the brass springs in circular openings in a heavy block of iron that was placed near the bottom of the case. The circular space prevented the spring's running down completely and kept it in check in case of a breakage. On the same arbor as the spring was placed a fusee which was not in the shape of a normal fusee but simply a flattish cone with a spiral groove cut on its surface. Another difference in the system was that, when the clock was fully wound, all the line was on the barrel in the movement instead of on the fusee, and as the line unwound, it began to fill the largest turn on the fusee and finished on the smallest.

This system was often used for shelf clocks with tall cases where

The movement of the Brewster & Ingrahams clock stripped down. The cast-iron backplate has containers for the brass mainsprings.

the springs and fusees would be located well away from the movement, but it also gave rise to the use of a new type of case which can be regarded as the first American design specially produced for a spring-driven clock. This was the 'Round Gothic', based on a design often used for bracket clocks in Britain during the Regency period and known as 'Lancet'. The American case is now known as a 'Beehive' by American collectors.

The design was first produced by Ray & Ingraham, and it lasted another thirty or forty years and was used by a number of other factories. The case differed from its British prototype in that the front opened to reveal the dial and pendulum, and the movement was fastened to the back of the case as on the Terry clocks. Unlike American cases that were to follow, the backboard had to be removed to get the movement out. Later American cases allowed the movement to be taken out after the dial had been removed, as on the OG. The curves in the top of the case were formed by a number of saw-cuts on the inside of the wood allowing it to be bent.

The Ingraham brothers played an important part in clock-development in America in the 1840s. They were not, however,

Left: The movement of a Brewster & Ingrahams thirty-hour Sharp Gothic, with brass springs. In this model the pins for operating the hammer also take the place of a cam. Right: The original design of the Brewster & Ingrahams Sharp Gothic case.

makers of movements but only of cases. Andrew, when in partnership with Benjamin Ray, had made the first of the Round Gothic or Beehive cases for E. C. Brewster, and Elias Ingraham was also a cabinet-maker who made clock-cases and designed the first Sharp Gothic case. The Sharp Gothic was one of the most popular cases ever used in America and resembles a section through the nave of a Gothic church. Two small pinnacles were placed at the top of the vertical sides and in the earliest form were plain cones, although in later years the pinnacles were decorated by turning. The base of the earliest Sharp Gothic cases was very low and plain but became higher and decorated by moulding as the years went by. The Sharp Gothic case differed from the Round Gothic in that it returned to the

A Brewster & Ingrahams Sharp Gothic thirty-hour clock with single-pin strike, brass mainsprings and ground-glass tablet.

Terry design of having the whole of the front of the clock exposed when the door was opened and therefore making it possible to remove the movement after the dial had been taken off. This system continued as a feature of American clock-cases until the turn of the century, when the fashion came in of having the movement fixed to the front of the case and the door at the back.

FUSEES AND DIRECT DRIVE

In 1844 the Ingraham brothers went into partnership with E. C. Brewster under the name of Brewster & Ingrahams, and while the firm lasted only eight years, it became the largest producer of clocks in the area and turned out some very interesting examples. The single-pin strike has been mentioned in connection with the OG movement, but it also featured in the Sharp Gothic case with a movement driven by brass springs. After the original Brewster clocks with reversed fusees came an improvement by Charles Kirk in 1843 whereby the back plate of the clock was made of iron and the casting provided two circular openings for housing the mainsprings to restrain them if they broke. This made the movement a lot smaller and did away with the complication of the fusees as the drive was direct. Another development at this period was to retain the reversed fusees but to connect them to the movement by special extension-pieces. This was patented by Boardman & Wells in 1847.

Brewster & Ingrahams produced a thirty-hour movement with brass springs that was a simplification of its predecessors. The general arrangement was on the usual principle of the OG but with four arbors on each side. The springs drove directly and had no containers, the back plate being of brass instead of iron. The wheels had five crossings, and the wheel that carried the pins for raising the hammer had one pin placed on each crossing. Instead of there being a cam or hoop for keeping the lifting-piece up while striking was in progress, the same five pins actuated a special wire attached to the lifting-piece and performed the same function. Locking was on the warning-wheel, and when the clock warned, the same pin that locked the train ran for about a quarter of a turn and was then held by another wire until it was released at the hour. At the rear of the arbor carrying the pin-wheel were five stumpy pins arranged like half of a lantern-pinion and which served to advance the count-wheel one tooth at every blow struck. The count-wheel was mounted centrally at the rear of the movement. This arrangement may have been devised to avoid infringing the Noble Jerome patent for striking-mechanism.

Brewster & Ingrahams clocks at this period often had tablets in ground glass rather than paint, but the effect is less pleasing. A clock of this period would have a lock and key to the door rather than the spring-catch or swivel that was fitted in later years. The firm often wrote its name on the dial, and the latter was held by a strip of wood below. Pendulum-bobs were heavier than on later clocks, a feature that made for better timekeeping.

Another design by the firm was the OG Gothic which resembled the Beehive, but instead of having the usual Gothic arch-termination above, a pair of reverse curves were introduced and the case terminated in a sharp point. A spring-driven Banjo clock was made and also circular wall clocks with 12-inch dials. These sometimes had their movements placed sideways and suggested the earlier clocks in New Hampshire. The movement-plates nearly always had a reinforcing-groove stamped in them that is characteristic of movements associated with Brewster.

By the late 1840s many firms were in the clock business using all kinds of movements, but in many instances the firms were not manufacturers but bought movements from specialist makers and cased them up in their own factories. The labels printed for them implied that the whole clock had been produced by the firm concerned, and in some instances the firm mentioned on the label had not even made the cases but was merely selling the products of different movement-shops and casemakers which had been combined. The complicated machinery necessary would not have made it economically viable for small firms to produce their own movements. A number of different makers used the reversed fusee with direct attachment to the movement. Others used the European-type fusee, particularly Chauncey Jerome. Jerome did not stick to the OG design but produced many other clocks, both weight- and spring-driven, and the reproduction of his 1853 catalogue is interesting in showing what was available at that time. Some of Jerome's best clocks were 12-inch dials with a drop-portion allowing the use of a longer pendulum and having movements with European fusees.

The problems associated with the use of fusees were, however, dramatically solved by Silas B. Terry, the youngest son of Eli, probably about 1847. He devised a method of hardening and tempering steel springs by the use of tallow and assigned it to Edward L. Dunbar, a supplier of clock accessories to the trade. The contract between Terry and Dunbar specified that the springs produced must not be sold to Chauncey Jerome. Dunbar was able to supply the new springs to various makers, but to begin with they were used in conjunction with the reversed fusee. Birge and Fuller discontinued the use of the Ives Wagon Spring in favour of the new method but continued to use the same type of case, consisting of a Sharp Gothic case on a broader base, a suggestion of the Case-on-Case style of sixty years previously. The base portion also had small pinnacles at the top corners to match those on the upper part of the case. These early Birge & Fuller clocks are rare in Britain; in fact it has been suggested that only one shipload of these clocks came over, but both types, the Wagon Spring and the reversed fusee type, are still met with, although naturally prices are very high.

The fusee began to give way to direct drive in the early 1850s, but before this occurred, competition had apparently become severe because two new case-designs came on the market. The first was from Brewster & Ingrahams and was a modification of their existing Sharp Gothic design by the addition of two free-standing columns on each side to which the pinnacles were applied. The other was the so-called 'Acorn' produced by J. C. Brown and formed to a fanciful shape by the use of bent laminated wood. Acorn clocks are found with reversed fusees in the bottom of the case and also attached to the movement by lugs as in the Boardman & Wells patent. Some of the reversed fusees are of wood. So far an example of the Ingraham free-standing columns has not been encountered in Britain, and the only Acorn seen is now in the British Museum. The short period of manufacture means that few can have been sent over.

The free-standing columns have also occurred on a wagon-spring clock with Sharp-Gothic-style case by Birge & Fuller. A Sharp Gothic clock by Silas B. Terry has twin pinnacles of the plain cone type on each side but no free-standing columns. This feature does not really add anything to the design. Another unusual item for the period is a Brewster & Ingrahams Beehive with a gesso and gold-leaf decoration all over the surface of the case. J. C. Brown in earlier years and E. N. Welch later were producing cases of the well-known Sharp Gothic shape but with the surface raised in a regular pattern now known as 'Ripple' or 'Piecrust'. Brown is even known for a 'Round Gothic' or 'OG Gothic' case such as was used by Brewster & Ingrahams with

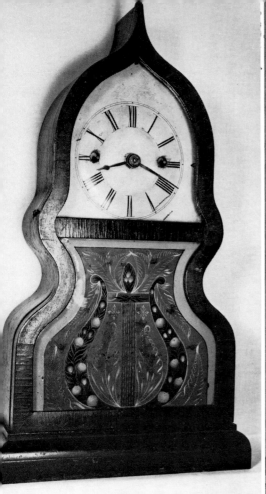 

Left: A thirty-hour fusee brass-movement clock in an 'Acorn' case by J. C. Brown, Forestville Clock Manufactory, Bristol, Connecticut, c. 1850. A mahogany veneered case with original reverse-painted glass. Right: A thirty-hour Wagon Spring by Birge & Fuller, Bristol, Connecticut, 1844–7. A double-steepled case with original glasses.

both free-standing columns and a ripple front. The effect is not so pleasing as the original design with plain veneer, but it shows what the various factories were doing to secure a greater share of the market.

One of the attractions in studying American clocks is to look out for familiar features in unusual combinations or occurring with the name of a manufacturer who was not known to have used them before.

Chauncey Jerome failed in 1856 and his business was taken over by the New Haven Clock Company. The latter firm became one of the most important in the business but continued to use the Jerome name on account of the goodwill value, usually in the form 'Jerome & Co'. Chauncey Jerome had produced a catalogue in 1852, and it is interesting to see what was being offered to the public at this early date. Three-quarters of the models offered are mantel spring-driven clocks, and only six out of a total of forty are weight-driven clocks, of the OG or similar types. The Beehive and the Sharp Gothic are included, and especially interesting is the number of clocks inlaid with mother-of-pearl. Most models are given names, a practice that was to continue in marketing American clocks. The Beehive is called 'Tudor', and others have such names as 'Jenny Lind', 'Prince Albert', 'Kossuth' and so on. Clocks with large dials for hanging on the wall are offered, and balance-controlled clocks are also there. The following year a more elaborate catalogue was produced, and this even included a marble case in French style. A number of the clocks were shown as being made of 'Papier Maiche' (*sic*). In view of the ban on Dunbar's selling springs to Jerome mentioned in his contract, it would appear that Jerome had penetrated some other source of supply and that probably more than one firm was then engaged in the business of making cheap steel springs.

A design that appears for the first time in the 1853 catalogue is the 'Cottage'. This proved popular with a number of makers in subsequent years and is virtually a scaled-down version of the OG for use on a mantel. The OG moulding has been eliminated, but the rectangular dial and case suggest the earlier model.

On account of the comparatively early date for the end of Jerome's business under his personal control, the number of true Jerome clocks with direct-driving springs cannot be great, and most of the examples seen will date from the period after the New Haven Clock Company had taken over. It is believed that the Seth Thomas Company did not make spring clocks until about 1860. By this time the direct-drive open spring was well established, and consequently one would not expect to find a Seth Thomas clock with any of the early features such as reversed fusees. Seth Thomas himself died in 1859, and his son Aaron succeeded him. Aaron quickly introduced many new models, and the firm published its first catalogue in 1863. This contained a number of weight clocks in OG or column-style cases, but it is important in being the earliest evidence of the sale of small timepieces only $7\frac{1}{2}$ inches or so high. Two styles are featured, the Cottage and the Octagon, and both lasted until the end of the century. Both could be supplied with alarm-work if desired, and the

Cottage was offered with the addition of striking-work in the catalogue of 1868. Many manufacturers offered clocks with the addition of alarm-work, as had been done with the OGs, and it usually meant that a certain number from the batch were given additional mechanism, although the plates of all the clocks were adapted to take it. This provides another feature for a collection, two specimens of the same model, one having alarm-work and the other one being without it. Strangely enough, the Sharp Gothic was not introduced into the Seth Thomas range until the 1870s.

As skill in making cheap steel springs increased, so did the number of clocks made to use them. Direct drive reduced the cost of movement manufacture. A timepiece could be made by using half the plate required for a striking-movement and re-locating the pillars. This often resulted in unsymmetrically placed winding-holes, and the latter feature is seen on all kinds of American spring clocks. It is an interesting exercise to work out what was in the mind of the designer when such a clock is encountered. The feature has precedents in the French clocks made during the Rococo period and also in the location of the winding-hole at the figure 2 on the Case on Case and the Banjo styles, but on some of the late-nineteenth-century factory clocks the idea appears to run wild.

A Sharp Gothic alarm by Jerome & Co (New Haven Clock Company). The plain paper in the back of the case would normally suggest a German origin, and the label on the rear of the glass is not often seen.

4   The Later Spring Clocks

The American Civil War broke out in 1861. It was not popular with Connecticut clock-factories because the Southern States were immediately eliminated from the potential market. The situation was now somewhat different from the mid-1830s when the Southern States had discouraged Yankee peddlers. (Improvements in transport had spread the Connecticut clock over a wide area.) It is not known to what extent the clock-factories were diverted to war production, but it was probably not very great. A photograph exists showing recruits drilling outside the Ansonia Brass and Battery Company mill in 1863, but it would be interesting to know exactly what the various firms did in the way of war production and how they coped with the drain of labour as men joined the army.

The Seth Thomas Company was busy during the early 1860s in building up a business in spring-driven clocks and issued its first catalogue in 1863, about half-way through the war. The Ingraham brothers had been in several partnerships since severing their connection with E. C. Brewster, but by 1861 Elias and his son were in control of the business, and new cases were designed. The 'Ionic' was a wall clock and was built up on two circles, one formed by the dial and the other forming the base with the pendulum-bob visible in its centre, while the 'Doric' was a mantel clock which was about the same height as the Sharp Gothic but with a much less pronounced point. These two designs were patented in 1861. From this time onwards, the Ingrahams abandoned the Sharp Gothic design which had been designed by Elias twenty years previously, although other firms continued to produce it. In 1864 Ingrahams produced and patented the 'Venetian' case. This was based on the Beehive except that the top was semicircular instead of forming a Gothic arch. The earliest examples had painted tablets, but by 1880 the clocks were being produced with plain glass and a mock gridiron pendulum, sometimes with metal leaves as a decoration over the bob. Some of the earlier clocks had the tinplate movement patented by Joseph Ives which was aimed at cheapening manufacture by using tinplate for the frames instead of brass and inserting brass bushes to take the pivots. Ives' roller-pinions and a new form of escapement based on the same idea were used to reduce friction.

In 1865 Ingrahams decided to make their own movements for the first time and opened a special shop to do this work. The Venetian and Doric cases continued in production until the turn of the century, although certain variations in the decoration of the basic cases lasted in some instances for only a few years. The Ionic was, however, still in vogue until the 1920s, although later models had plain glass in the base. Most of the Ingrahams range could be obtained with one-day or eight-day movements.

In spite of the long time that the various models were in production, Ingraham clocks are rare in Britain. This is not the case with the earlier Brewster & Ingrahams clocks, but only those of the E. Ingraham Company that was established about 1860. This is a pity, for some of the models were very attractive. The clocks show the trend of future design in that the dials are surrounded by a circular bezel instead of being printed on a larger piece of metal which was square or of a suitable shape to fit under the pointed roof.

A perusal of old catalogues of the late-nineteenth century will show that most firms were making very similar models often with only detail differences but with different names. A Gilbert catalogue of 1875 contains many models that can be described as traditional, i.e. with a smooth veneered surface to the cases and coloured tablets in front of the pendulum, but already the plain glass with the mock compensated pendulum had appeared, and cases were being decorated with applied carving or turning. The firm's own versions of the Venetian and the Doric appear, but the models bear different names.

ANSONIA CLOCKS AND OTHERS

The Ansonia Clock Company grew out of a brass-manufactory in Ansonia, Connecticut, but in 1877 it was decided to separate the clock business into a separate firm instead of running it as a sideline to the company's main business. The Ansonia Clock Company was

Left: An eight-day Sharp Gothic from the Ansonia Brass Company, 1854–69.
Right: Its movement.

established in a large factory in Brooklyn, New York, in 1878 but it was burned down in 1880. A new factory was built in 1881, and two years later all operations were moved there from Ansonia.

More Ansonia clocks are seen in Britain today than those of any other American producer. Their speciality was marble or imitation marble cases to compete with the French clocks that were being sold at the time in Britain and elsewhere. A new eight-day movement was designed by the firm and appeared in a variety of cases. There were large open mainsprings and pegs mounted in the plate to restrain them if they broke, and the striking was a successor to the idea of the Brewster single-pin strike. On the Ansonia clock the cam had, however, two slots for locking and two pins for raising the hammer, but it still eliminated the adjustment necessary when assembling to ensure that the train locked the instant after the hammer had fallen. This movement appears not only in many different models but also behind many different types of dial. It is often seen with a visible escapement in a sunken centre-portion of the dial as on the French clocks, sometimes even with stones for pallets, but it is usually possible to detect the clock's origin from a distance as the winding-holes are in the chapter ring at 4 and 8 rather than in the sunken portion of the dial as on the French clocks. In addition, many of the clocks have the trademark on the dial, a letter 'A' in a square surrounded by a diamond, and usually the full name of the firm round the extreme lower edge of the dial. The brass from which the movement is made is of a very distinctive yellow colour. Further differences from normal American practice are that the count-wheel has continuous drive from a pinion instead of being advanced one tooth at a time, and a French type of pendulum-bob with the rating-nut in the middle is provided. This bob simply hooks on to the pendulum-wire by means of a short brass stem and does not possess the double claw that is found on French pendulums.

In its earliest form the new movement retained the escapement on the front plate in true American style and also possessed stopwork to limit the range through which the springs could be wound. It was made with lugs at the rear to be fastened to the back of the case. The form in which it is best known is with the escapement between the plates or arranged in front of the dial. Provision is made for regulating the clock by means of a square over the figure 12 after the clock has been brought nearly to time by means of the rating-nut in the pendulum-bob. This is the same idea as that used in the Brocot suspension found in almost all French clock-movements and operates by varying the length of the effective part of the suspension-spring. The winding-key was made with a small extension at the rear which would fit the square over the 12, and such keys are still obtainable and are often known as 'Ansonia Keys'. The winding-squares in the movement are large on account of the strong mainsprings, usually size 12, and Ansonia and other eight-day springs should be treated with great respect.

The 1880 catalogue for Ansonia shows a range of imitation marble clocks, many of them being enamelled iron. Some firms specialized in producing these iron cases for the clock-factories, and the stoving-process which they underwent produced a hard black finish that retains its lustre today, although unfortunately many cases are now showing signs of rust penetrating here and there. By the time the 1886 catalogue was published, clocks in the French style had taken a much more prominent place. Not only were the imitation marble clocks well to the fore but also cases which included

A late movement with rack strike by the Waterbury Clock Company, used in imitation-marble cases as well as other models.

An Ansonia iron-cased clock with the 1882 movement.

statuettes such as had been popular in France in the early years of the nineteenth century. The 1880 catalogue does not illustrate any visible escapements. The 1886 catalogue features them extensively, but they were charged extra on the marble clocks. The bronze clocks with statuettes were supplied only with visible escapements. The 1886 catalogue also includes a number of bronze statuettes and other ornaments for displaying beside the clocks. Dials were $5\frac{1}{2}$ inches in diameter, and other features of the clocks were half-hour strike, cathedral gong on sounding-board, French solid brass sash (bezel), beveled plate-glass and black enamelled, white porcelain or gilt dial.

The half-hour strike was usually arranged on American clocks by having an extra tail to the hammer which was raised by the cam that was used for releasing the striking-train at the hour. As the hammer was below the movement, the cam would be at the correct place half an hour after releasing the striking-train. Half-hours were therefore sounded without unlocking the striking-train, and this saved a certain amount of power and made a simpler count-wheel possible. In spite of this, clocks are encountered where the striking-train *is* released for the half-hours and the count-wheel is formed with a very long, slender tooth between the groups of teeth representing the hours. This is a weakness, and if the slender teeth get bent, the striking can fail. The Waterbury Company arranged its clocks to strike a single blow at the half-hour on a bell, to distinguish it from the gong used for the hours. The gongs on these American movements resembled French gongs and were in complete contrast to those used on the OGs and other typical American designs. They upheld American tradition, though, in being placed below the movement instead of at the rear as on French clocks. The catalogue of 1886 also mentions slow strike which was in complete contrast to the traditional American clocks. The term 'cathedral gong' appears to have originated in the mid-1880s, but other firms used it as well as Ansonia.

The 1880 Ansonia catalogue contains three models which we would call 'Four Glass' today but which in later years were known as 'Crystal Regulators' in America. The name of the model was 'Symbol', and it included the pendulum often found on other models which suggested temperature compensation on both the mercury and gridiron principles at the same time. The gong was at the rear, and apparently the standard eight-day movement was used. A small scale below the pendulum indicated the amplitude of the swing. By 1886 these three models had disappeared and been replaced by the solitary 'Symbol Extra' which had its gong slightly higher, a visible escapement and decorated hands. Perhaps these clocks were before their time because twenty years later Ansonia was to publish a complete catalogue devoted to Crystal Regulators, showing cases with many different forms of decoration. The later clocks have been completely redesigned with a smaller movement that more resembled its French prototype, and the dummy compensation-pendulums have been replaced by the typical French pendulum for this type with two tubes of mercury. The gong has also gone behind the movement, and the scale below the pendulum has been omitted. Jewelled visible escapements are fitted to practically every model, and the dial-diameter has been reduced from 6 inches or 5 inches to $4\frac{1}{2}$ inches.

To return to 1880. A number of wooden clocks are shown which are now known as 'Walnuts'. They embody the traditional American features of the movement fastened to the back of the case with a glazed door-opening up the entire front, but the plainness of the original Sharp Gothics or Beehives is lacking. The case fronts are

A Crystal Regulator by Ansonia, *c.* 1900. The rear view shows the French-type movement, rack strike and mercury pendulum.

spread out beyond the door and decorated with carving or applied ornaments in the typical late-Victorian style. These clocks are fitted with the standard eight-day movement, and it obviously made for efficient production when the same movement could be included in so many different cases. By 1886 the number of Walnuts had increased, and included among them are more highly decorated versions of the Sharp Gothic, Beehive and other clocks resembling Ingraham's Doric and Venetian. Only one page is devoted to the traditional American clocks, and these are Cottage and Cottage Extra one-day time, one-day alarm and one-day strike, and eight-day strike with a corresponding alarm model. There are also small Sharp Gothic one-day time, one-day alarm and one-day strike, and a one-day OG with alarm as an optional extra.

Particular attention has been given to the Ansonia catalogues, but much the same story is told by those of other large factories, except that other firms show more of the traditional types. Ingrahams are making a slow start with the imitation marble clocks, but everyone is producing the Walnut type in various styles. It is somewhat a matter for surprise that so few of these are seen today compared with the much older clocks of the traditional type. Possibly the designs were too highly spiced for the tastes of the 1920s and after, and many of the clocks could have become casualties then while the older clocks, being plainer, have survived. Possibly the coloured tablets of the older clocks may have been responsible for their survival.

Ansonia appears to have been the trend-setter in the eighties, and the catalogue includes not only complete clocks but also a range of spare parts of all kinds. One page of the 1886 catalogue contains two models only, under the heading of 'cabinet clocks'. These are important because they provided the basic idea for development in the new century, i.e. a wooden case with the movement fixed to the front of it in the same way as the imitation marble clocks were constructed. The door was at the back, and the standard movement with rear pendulum was used. One of these models, known as the 'Tivoli', must have been very popular in Britain as examples are frequently met with. The case was plain wood of a medium brown (the catalogue actually states black walnut or mahogany), and although there was a certain amount of carving, and turned pillars were placed beside the dial, the decoration was not carried to excess. The other model, called 'Tunis', has not so far been noted.

WELCH, SPRING & CO.

In order to preserve chronological order, it is now necessary to consider the firm of Welch, Spring & Co. E. N. Welch was a successful businessman who had acquired the factory of J. C. Brown and become a very important clock-manufacturer. Solomon C. Spring was interested in fine woodwork and produced cases for other makers as well as movements and parts. A few clocks were sold under his own name, but they are now rare. In 1868 Welch and Spring formed a company, the idea being to manufacture clocks of a higher quality than those produced by Welch's factory. Many of the earlier models incorporated calendar-work and were weight-driven, but in 1877 Spring turned his attention to shelf clocks. There had previously been some models called 'Italian' which were loosely

Left: A mantel clock by Welch, Spring & Co, *c.* 1880. The pendulum suggests three glass tubes of mercury for compensation, but it is of metal. Right: The 'Patti' by Welch, Spring & Co, 1880 catalogue.

based on Ingraham's Venetian and not very far removed from the appearance of a traditional American clock.

The first two years of production saw the appearance of several models, both wall and mantel clocks, but in 1879 came the most famous of all, the 'Patti'. This was named after the famous singer Adelina Patti, for it was the practice of the firm to choose names of famous musicians or composers for their models. The case of the Patti was the subject of a patent, and the underlying idea was to produce the parts accurately enough by machine so that they were interchangeable and could be assembled without the use of glue. The case had glass sides and glass front with the movement fastened to the back of the case, but the movement, as well as the case design, showed some novel features. It was provided with the club-tooth escapement which had been used on some Welch clocks previously, while the pendulum-suspension was on a wire loop like that usually fitted to a cuckoo-clock. The mainsprings were double and, unlike many American clocks, had their clicks fastened to the front plate. The escapement was between the plates, but the depthing of the pallets was adjusted by mounting the pivots in holes in movable brass discs, which was the method Terry used in his Pillar-and-Scroll clock save that Terry's pallets ran on a fixed stud. The plates of the movement were comparatively small, and the cut-out portion formed the pattern of a St Andrew's Cross. The movement was subsequently re-designed with a spring suspension and the regulation arranged by means of a square, as on the Ansonias previously mentioned. The plates were much thicker than on the usual American movement, and the clock was provided with a decorative pendulum having a piece of glass in the centre of the bob. Striking was on a bell rather than on a gong, and the bell was placed below the movement in the traditional American position.

The Patti clock in its case was $18\frac{1}{2}$ inches high, but a smaller model, only $10\frac{1}{2}$ inches high, was also made which is now known as the 'Baby Patti'. The smaller clocks are known with striking-work and as timepieces. The pendulum was hung from the back on the latter model. The workmanship was of good quality, and the clocks cost several times more to make than the average clock of the time, while they sold for only a few dollars more. Inevitably the company could not continue, and it was sold to the E. N. Welch Company in 1884, which included the stock in its 1885 catalogue and even continued to produce some of the models. The Welch firm came into the hands of a receiver in 1893, and all production was suspended.

The Patti, in spite of having a lot of applied decoration, is quite an attractive clock, especially in the miniature version. Unfortunately the market was not prepared to absorb a quality production, and the design was going against the main stream of development at the period. Such a clock would be well worth adding to one's collection.

At the opposite end of the scale as far as case-design was concerned were the 'Oaks', sometimes known as 'Sidewhiskers' or 'Gingerbreads'. The basis for the design was the Walnut type of case, but the front was spread out into a wide area and the wood decorated with an embossed pattern produced in moulds under the influence of steam and pressure. These clocks appeared at the end of the 1890s, and as they coincided with the period of the Spanish American War, the designs often had contemporary themes including such subjects as Admiral Dewey, President McKinley, the battleship *Maine*, which was mysteriously sunk at Havana, and so on. These clocks are now regarded as kitchen clocks, and that was probably their function when new. Although they have eight-day movements, the quality of the case does not approach that of the Walnuts. Perhaps the most famous design of all was the Ingraham 'Gila', which incorporated a storm-gauge and a thermometer in the case and the day of the month shown outside the main series of figures. This is one of the few Ingraham clocks seen in Britain today.

WALL CLOCKS

Before leaving the nineteenth century, consideration ought to be given to wall clocks. In Britain, the OG was nearly always used as a wall clock although the original design was intended for a shelf clock, hence the flat bottom without any veneer. When a clock is intended to be hung on the wall, the bottom surface is very prominent and needs polish or some finish to relieve it. The fusee drop-dials by Jerome have already been mentioned, and the inspiration for these clocks was undoubtedly the well-known 'English Dial' which was made in great numbers during the nineteenth century. Ingraham's Ionic was a further development in this direction, but although the Ionic design was copied by other

The movement of a miniature wall clock by Seth Thomas (after 1869), showing the lyre-shaped plates often used by the firm.

An Ansonia 12-inch dial with the escapement between the plates, the pendulum supported at the top of the case.

An eight-day Beehive movement by Jerome & Co (New Haven Clock Company). The 'Y' shape of the centre portion of the front plate is characteristic of this firm.

firms and given other names, the most popular design for wall-clocks in America is the so called 'Schoolhouse'. This is basically a 12-inch dial with a trunk below it usually longer than on English clocks and with a circular or octagonal surround to the dial. The trunk can be glazed for most of the available area or decorated with inlay and have only a small opening to give access to the pendulum bob.

The earliest record of a clock of this type is in the William Gilbert catalogue of 1875. The Seth Thomas catalogue of 1868 has a derivative of the Ionic design called 'Office', but that company's catalogue for 1879 has the proper 'Drop Octagon' (Schoolhouse) illustrated. Most of the clocks seen in Britain today have movements by the New Haven Clock Company, and there are five examples in this company's catalogue for 1880. The New Haven catalogue for 1888–90 shows several more variations on the theme, as well as more versions of the Ionic. Some of the dial-clocks have the day of the month shown outside the hour figures. The New Haven movement usually has the company's trademark stamped on the front plate, but even when this is absent, the movements can be recognized by the fact that the spaces cut in the front plate leave the form of a letter 'Y'. The Ansonia catalogue for 1880 does not feature a large number of drop octagons, but the version with a longer trunk that came a little later became a real speciality of Ansonia, and many such clocks were sent to Britain. The name 'Regulator' is sometimes placed on the glass, and some of the clocks had a scale to show the amplitude of the swing, but the name 'Regulator' is purely for sales promotion. A true Regulator would be weight-driven and have a dead-beat escapement and no striking-work.

A clock of this type of somewhat higher quality was the 'Verdi' produced by Welch, Spring & Co in 1877 and made by them and later by E. N. Welch up to 1893. This clock had a dead-beat escapement and a seconds-hand, and although it was fitted with striking, the warning-wheel was given a large number of teeth to slow the striking down from the usual American speed.

A number of American firms produced their own version of the Vienna Regulator but with spring drive. These clocks have pendulums with wooden rods that do not vary greatly through changes in temperature. These clocks were also produced by German factories, particularly in the shorter version, but the shorter type do not seem to have been so important in America although versions of the design do appear.

The next catalogue which gives an idea of what the public were buying is that of the St Louis Clock and Silverware Company, produced at the time of the World's Fair held in that city in 1904. Large numbers of Oaks were shown, and it appears that the method of selling was to offer them in groups with so many clocks in a group all different. In this way the factory could guarantee sales of the less popular models as well as the popular ones. The average price was about $4 per clock. Most of the large factories such as Ingraham, William Gilbert, Seth Thomas and Waterbury were supplying them. The height of the clocks varied between 22 and 24 inches, which is somewhat tall for a mantel clock but not so bad if the old-fashioned high Victorian kitchen mantelpiece is considered. Decorated pendulum-bobs were the fashion.

The same catalogue shows many Crystal Regulator designs not only by Ansonia but also by Seth Thomas and Waterbury. They are described as 'the most popular clocks on the market today'. With prices eight to ten times as much as the 'Oaks', one wonders if this were true. The bronze clocks with statuettes produced by Ansonia were joined by some similar models from Waterbury. Imported cases of genuine French black marble were provided with Ansonia movements, as were cases of Brazilian or Belgian onyx. The iron cases to imitate black marble are still offered but have been joined by imitations in wood and 'marbleized' finishes. The usual factories share in these.

A new type of clock case is the Royal Bonn porcelain. It is described as Art Nouveau and seems to have been mostly for Ansonia movements with visible escapements. Waterbury provided one or two. The clocks are not often seen today as their nature makes them fragile. Collectors usually want them only if the cases are absolutely perfect.

A survey of the position regarding spring clocks is given by the Waterbury catalogue of 1908–9. There is a large selection of Crystal Regulators with visible escapements and mercury pendulums. While all the models are shown with visible escapements, they can be supplied without them at the same price. There are a large number of clocks in cast bronze using the same or a similar movement, and this movement also appears in a very large selection of imitation marble cases in wood or enamelled iron. An important innovation is the use of this movement in wooden cases much plainer than the usual clocks then being supplied but probably aimed at the British market

Jerome Octagon Prize Model
eight–day, *c.* 1870

Ansonia Cabinet clock Peak
Model eight–day, *c.* 1880–1900

Ansonia thirty-day Round
Head Office Regulator, *c.* 1900

Ansonia Queen Elizabeth
Regulator eight–day, *c.* 1900

Left: A small timepiece by the William Gilbert Clock Company. The style goes back to the 1850s, but the clock is probably about 1890. The mainspring is outside the plates, facilitating its replacement. Right: An Ansonia eight-day visible-escapement movement in a Royal Bonn porcelain case, *c*. 1904.

as the names of the models are 'Essex', 'Suffolk', 'Kent' and similar titles. These clocks represent a further development of the 'Cabinet Clocks' in the Ansonia catalogue of 1886. The movements supplied in many of the clocks mentioned above, particularly the wooden-cased ones aimed at the British market, have the winding-holes nearer the centre of the dial which is a great improvement.

Oaks are slightly less numerous, but the Sharp Gothic and the Waterbury version of the Ingraham Venetian are still being offered. These items probably represent stock that has remained unsold for years. Octagon drops and other wall clocks are offered in a number of models, and even two of the Oaks have been developed into wall clocks. There are several models of the drop-dial type of Regulator and a series of shorter, spring-driven Vienna Regulators obviously made to compete with the German factories. These types are very rare in Britain, where the German factories were having it all their own way at the time. The size of the American clocks corresponds to the German ones, but there is virtually little other resemblance. The larger, spring-driven Vienna Regulators are not like German models either, except for two of them named 'Dresden' and 'Leipsic'. Many of the models could be supplied with thirty-day movements, and a choice of oak, walnut or mahogany was given for the cases.

Probably one of the last types of clock to be exported to Britain in large numbers was the Lancet case by William Gilbert. These clocks were freely based on the Regency style bracket clocks, and the movements were not unlike the Ansonia model of 1881, but regulation was by means of the square over the dial only, and the pendulum-bob was a plain casting with no rating-nut. The dials are nearly always provided with Arabic figures and bear the word 'Gilbert' under the 12. Some have the firm's trademark also. Clocks in the styles of the 1920s seem to have made little impression on the British market, for most clocks of this type now met with are of British or German manufacture.

MARKETING, AT HOME AND ABROAD

The marketing of all these clocks required some careful organization. Chauncey Jerome established an agent in Liverpool to handle his business, but there grew up after this a class of businessmen known as 'American importers' who handled all kinds of American goods as well as clocks and who were located mostly in the City of London. For example, Brewster & Ingrahams operated through agents at 13 Walbrook (N. L. Brewster) from 1848, and there was Holloway & Co at 128/9 Minories. More will be said about this firm in a subsequent chapter.

It was during the 1860s that factory production of clocks of the American type began in Germany, and the first firm to open an office in London was Philipp Haas & Söhne of St Georgen, Black Forest, in 1871. The German competition had an effect in America, for, beginning in 1874 with Seth Thomas, American factories began opening their own offices in London. E. N. Welch came in 1876, and Ansonia made Holloway & Co their agents at the time of their reorganization and move to Brooklyn in 1879. In 1883 they opened their own office. Jerome/New Haven appeared in 1884, William Gilbert in 1891 and Ingraham in 1900. It does not appear that the Waterbury Company had any London office in the nineteenth century, but by 1908 they were established in Glasgow.

The catalogues which we have been considering began in a very modest way. The earliest Jerome of 1852 had very crude illustrations indeed, and the one of 1853 shows little improvement. Recent research indicates that the clocks shown were not all of Jerome's own make but included certain models by Birge Peck and other firms.

The Seth Thomas of 1863 has much better illustrations, while the subsequent ones are much better drawn and about the turn of the century include photographs. The early Jerome catalogue inaugurated the practice of giving each model a name, and this idea was developed by other firms. Sometimes a series of similar models was given names bearing the same initial letter. Others might be named after a series of rivers or towns. The New Haven Clock Company catalogue of 1888–90 did its utmost to make the business of selling clocks as easy as possible. It contained a comprehensive telegraph code so that complicated orders could be telegraphed in very few words, and detailed information was given on the weight and cubic capacity of various consignments, together with the number of clocks packed into a case. The customer could choose between bells or gongs on striking clocks, and half-hour striking could be added if desired. Most models could have alarm-work added for a small charge.

Broadly speaking, the American spring-driven pendulum clocks which are found in Britain all date from before 1914. Even as late as 1908 many of the models have a very old-fashioned look, as shown by the Waterbury catalogue for that year. The American collector has a much wider range, for many of the models produced seem to have remained on the home market, especially those which were in the upper-price bracket. The spring-pendulum clocks available in Britain would cover a period from, say, 1850 to 1910, about sixty years in all. The American collector could add thirty years to the end of this period, but in the years of the Depression and of the beginning of the electric clock as a domestic timekeeper the production of pendulum clocks greatly diminished. The popularity of radio made striking clocks less popular as the striking would interfere with the programme. Clocks with balances were not dependent on being set to a correct level, and they were also cheaper and could be thrown away when needing attention, as a replacement was quite inexpensive. The realm of the pendulum mantel or wall clock, however, does cover some of the most interesting of American clocks and is probably the most popular field for present-day collectors.

Illustrations from Ansonia's 1880 catalogue. Left column: Carriage clocks – from top to bottom, 'Peep o'Day', 'Companion' and 'Brilliant'. Right column: Balance clocks – from top to bottom, 'Princess', 'Peep o'Day' (their first drum alarm) and 'Planet'.

5   The Balance Clocks

The balance was the earliest form of controller on mechanical clocks, but unfortunately it has no set period of swing and consequently, without a balance-spring, varies its rate in accordance with the power being supplied to the train. It began as a horizontal bar known as a 'foliot' which was used on turret clocks and also on the earliest domestic clocks, but later it was modified into a heavy wheel whereby the mass was more evenly spread. With the advent of the mainspring as motive-power, clocks became smaller, and the balance was likewise reduced in size. After the invention of the pendulum, the balance became obsolete for weight clocks.

As soon as the pendulum clock began to be used, a serious disadvantage became apparent. It had to be set to a correct level before it would function satisfactorily, and if the level were too inaccurate, the clock would not go at all. At this time people were used to table clocks and watches that were self-starting and did not have to be set to a certain level, but they were very inaccurate when compared with pendulum clocks. The application of the balance-spring (hairspring) late in the seventeenth century produced a timekeeper much more reliable than the previous ones, although it could not compete with the pendulum for accuracy.

The verge escapement was still used, and it was not until the eighteenth century that other escapements were invented that showed an improvement on it. First came the cylinder, to be followed by the duplex, the virgule and the lever, to mention only the better-known types, but it is interesting to note that all these escapements were for application to watches, and the portable clock was very much in the background. The highest development in this direction was the carriage watch, a timekeeper rather larger than the pocket watch which could be hung in a carriage but which in essential was a verge watch fitted with a balance-spring and possibly the additions of striking- and alarm-work.

PORTABLE CLOCKS

About the beginning of the nineteenth century Napoleon's officers were using portable clocks that were virtually carriage watches brought up to date, but they were expensive, and comparatively few were made. Thomas Mudge had made a watch for Queen Charlotte with the lever escapement, but he did not take a great deal of interest in his invention, and other men were to do the necessary development before this escapement became really popular. The Rack Lever was introduced in the late-eighteenth century and while not extremely accurate, would have been a useful escapement for portable clocks. By about 1840 the detached lever of Mudge had been brought to a state of development sufficient for it to be used extensively on pocket watches, and the famous English Lever became a byword for accurate time-measurement.

All these developments were being brought about by watchmakers. The portable clock as such was still very much as it had been – a verge watch-movement slightly larger than the usual size mounted in a small wooden case. These little clocks are known today as 'Sedan Chair clocks', but whether it was the custom to provide sedan chairs with clocks is not known. The name, however, seems to have come to stay. In the early-nineteenth century a new variation was the 'Pendule de Voyage', now known as the 'carriage clock', which became extremely popular as the nineteenth century wore on and people began to travel to an extent they had never done before. The carriage clock was essentially a clock for travelling rather than a clock to be displayed in a carriage, and it was provided with a leather carrying-case to protect it from the rigours of the journey. A panel could be slid up to reveal the dial when travelling, but the real function of the clock was to stand beside the traveller's bed, and it was generally provided with an alarm or repeating-mechanism to wake him at the correct hour or tell him the time during the night. These clocks were at first in the very high price-bracket, but as the century wore on, cheaper versions that were only timepieces were produced, and the cylinder escapement also helped to reduce the cost. Naturally the performance was inferior to that of the lever. The standard of workmanship of carriage clocks was nearer to that of watch-work rather than clock-work.

The all-conquering lever escapement of the 1840s was the old British type with sharp teeth. The points of the teeth were very delicate and were subject to wear, so later the club-tooth lever was introduced whereby the end of the tooth was solid and shared the impulse with the pallet. This form of escapement lasted until the present time when mechanical watches are giving way to quartz.

The same idea was used for a pendulum clock escapement by E. N. Welch on small timepieces and also by Welch, Spring & Co. This escapement was a patent of 1870 and was designed for pendulum clocks, but clocks with balances and lever escapements were by that time well known in America, and it is necessary to go back some twenty years to trace their origin.

Eli Terry's last patent was granted in 1845 and consisted of a method of supporting a balance in a clock-movement. It is not clear what Terry hoped to achieve by this mechanism for there was the difficulty at that time of providing a hairspring to be considered, and such a clock would probably be an inferior timekeeper to one with a pendulum. The principle involved was to support the balance-arbor by means of a stirrup which itself was supported from a bar above, either being rigidly fixed to it, in which case the bar would run on pivots in holes in the frame, or else being connected to the bar by a spring, in which case the bar would be fixed to the frame. As the balance vibrated, the pivot would roll on the inner side of the stirrup and cause it to move to and fro. Terry's patent specified that the stirrup supported the balance-arbor at its centre of gravity, but allowance was made for two stirrups if desired. Several clocks with this mechanism are known, both weight- and spring-driven, and the earliest is a wooden movement of the usual Terry shelf clock type. The balance is usually visible, and seconds-hands are included, but the only real advantage seems to be that the balance beats seconds. The clocks would not have been cheap, so the invention is not an attempt to cheapen cost of production. While the same result could probably have been achieved with a pendulum, although one that beat twice a second would be needed if the overall size is not to be too great, the clocks do not have to be set to a correct level. They are much too big to be really portable.

The Terry clocks were made by Eli's son S. B. Terry, and another clock by this maker has been noted where the balance is placed horizontally below the movement. This clock is somewhat later and is a timepiece only but has the novelty of having the mainspring outside the plates so that it can be replaced without having to take the entire movement to pieces. This clock would have been much cheaper to make than the previous ones, but the sole gain seems to be that the clock did not have to be accurately levelled.

Terry's experiments are interesting, but they did not show the way to the commercial production of balance-clocks. This needed cheap steel mainsprings which were also pioneered by S. B. Terry and the idea sold to Edward Dunbar in 1847. Not only did the steel mainspring form an important part of the conception, but the balance-spring too needed to be manufactured in quantity at a realistic price. William B. Barnes developed a movement about 1848 and in 1849 he formed a partnership with Ebenezer Hendrick to produce it. These movements were sold to Jerome, J. C. Brown and others who provided the cases. Jerome's catalogue of 1852 includes them under the heading of 'Detached Lever Timepieces, for vessels, cars, etc'. They are offered in mahogany, walnut, zebra and rosewood cases and with dials 6 inches, 8 inches and 10 inches in diameter. Another model with a 9-inch dial ran for eight days. The latter may have been a product of Noah Pomeroy, who was in business only as a movement-maker and is known for his eight-day marine type.

The Detached Lever in the title refers to the fact that for most of its swing the balance is not influenced by the movement but is quite free. At that time a number of rack lever watches were still in use, and it was necessary to distinguish the new type as it was an improvement on the rack lever. The mention of vessels and cars (railway carriages) indicates the main use to which the new balance clocks would be put. From 1830 onwards the railway system had begun to develop in the United States, and already before this time there was a well established system of steamboats on most of the larger rivers. The Mississippi in particular was well known for its passenger-services, and the voyage from New Orleans to St Louis or up the Ohio river to Pittsburgh would last many days, so a clock for the use of passengers was a real necessity. The voyages up the Hudson from New York to Albany or from New York up Long Island Sound were not so long, but the clocks were just as useful. Sometimes the early balance clocks are called 'Marine or Locomotive', and they would have been useful in the cabs of locomotives on the early railroads. In the 1850s the USA was having to import nearly all the watches it needed, which made them expensive, and a good timekeeper was necessary for running a railroad. It was much later in history that the locomotive crew would be issued with watches.

The usual case for the lever-movements was in the shape of an octagon with applied veneer. The movement had lugs for fastening it to the back of the case in the usual American fashion, and the balance was between the plates, usually at the top. Jerome's early

Left: The circular version of the 'Marine or Locomotive', by the New Haven Clock Company, late-nineteenth century. Right: A 'Marine or Locomotive', c. 1870.

catalogues even show lever-movements in wooden or papier mâché cases resembling those of mantel clocks, but the majority of the type were sold in the usual octagonal or circular form, and most of the large firms produced them.

The Seth Thomas catalogue of 1863 does not include them, but by 1879 the firm was offering a good selection with dials of various sizes and in some instances the choice of striking or alarm as an addition. Production began in 1865, when a saw-mill was converted into a special movement-shop to manufacture balance-movements, and this shop was used until 1879. The 1879 catalogue also includes a 'Chronometer Lever' which is offered in two sizes and has a porcelain dial, steel pinions and chronometer-balance and is jewelled. The case is of cast brass, and this provided the model for the ships' bell clocks that the firm made. Some of the later models had cases only of tinplate, but the ships' bell clock was very popular and was made up to 1940.

The Welch catalogue for 1885 contains an elaboration of the normal ship's clock. It was patented in the USA in 1879, in Great Britain, Canada and France in the same year and in Germany in 1880. The clock could be supplied in a nickel or a brass case, and great care had been taken to turn out a very fine movement. The hands could be turned backwards if necessary for daily changes in longitude without interfering with the strike.

Not only were the marine clocks popular with many makers, but everyone offered them in several sizes. Even the Gilbert catalogue of 1875, which offered a more limited choice than some of the factories, listed 4-, 6- and 8-inch lever-clocks with the wooden surround, two models including alarm and two including striking. Ingrahams offered many lever-clocks in 1880, but they preferred a circular wooden surround to the octagonal one, although they offered a limited choice in the latter. The type still features in the Waterbury catalogue of 1908–9.

Some of the eight-day models will be found to possess two mainsprings. The two winding-holes on the dial give the impression that the clock is fitted with striking mechanism, which is not the case. The idea was used by Breguet in his marine chronometers, and its main purpose is to overcome the disadvantage of using an extremely large mainspring. Such a spring would not only be of large diameter but its thickness would have an effect on the design of the case. By using two mainsprings of more moderate size, it is possible to use springs that are suitable for other models and avoid the excessive wear on the pivots that a single large mainspring would produce. The use of standard material also helps to keep costs down. There is an additional bonus in the arrangement of the springs on each side of the arbor that they drive, for each spring forces the arbor in an opposite direction and so cancels out the wear on the pivots. If one of the springs breaks, the damage to the movement would be less severe than if a very large single spring were to break, and when one spring is being wound, the other acts as maintaining power if barrels are not provided.

An exception to the popularity of the 'Marine' is found in the catalogue of the Terry Clock Company of Pittsfield, Massachusetts, issued in 1885. This firm was owned by three grandsons of Eli Terry and had begun business in 1867, moving to Pittsfield in 1880. It was taken over by creditors in 1888. While not manufacturing the balance clock with a wooden surround, the Company produced a number of balance movements in metal cases. An important feature of these clocks was that many models were provided with luminous dials made under a British patent of 1877 granted to William Balmain of Ventnor, Isle of Wight. The patent had also been taken out in many other countries and in the United States in 1882. While the dials of luminous clocks are often black, the illustrations in this catalogue suggest that the clocks had white dials, and such a clock turning up today would be a real collector's item. The luminosity would, however, have expired after almost a hundred years.

The early movements for marine clocks were provided with a solid lever and the British form of sharp-toothed scapewheel. A later development was the introduction of the pin-pallet escapement where the pallets consist merely of two pins and the impulse is given as these pins run over the oblique edges of the scapewheel teeth. This form of escapement was invented for watches as long ago as 1798 by Louis Perron of Besançon and provided for 'draw' to prevent a disturbance causing the lever to unlock at the wrong time. It required a certain amount of care in manufacture and did not become popular, although it was modified by Adolf Lange of Glashütte in Saxony in the early years of his factory and used by him for watch movements. The escapement became really popular after Georg Friedrich Roskopf had modified it with a view to producing watches really cheaply, and it was also applied to balance clocks.

ALARMS, DRUMS AND NOVELTIES

The alarm-clock has been a necessity of life for centuries and many of the earlier pendulum clocks made in America were fitted with alarm-work in addition to the striking. In the wooden clock era a number of makers produced shelf clocks with wooden wheels having no strike but alarm only, and after the brass movement OG began to become established, it could usually be purchased with alarm-mechanism for a small extra sum. With the cheapening of steel springs and the advent of the small pendulum clocks, many makers produced small mantel clocks with alarm but with no striking-mechanism, and it has been mentioned that many of the clocks of the Marine type could be supplied with alarm if desired. Rapid economic development in the USA meant a large number of immigrants after the Civil War and a need to provide alarm-clocks even cheaper than were being supplied at the time. The problem was solved by doing away with the wooden case and using a less elaborate version of the type of movement used in the Marine clock with alarm-mechanism added. The new cases were made from sheet metal and usually given a finish in nickel, hence the name 'Nickel Alarm' that is sometimes applied to them.

Traditionally the drum alarm-clock with metal case that has been

A Seth Thomas alarm in a bronze case. The alarm runs for twenty minutes if desired.

a familiar object in the home for generations was introduced by Seth Thomas in 1876. The date of the patent was 24th October 1876, and the clock had a circular metal case with bell and carrying-loop above, a small bracket below to support the clock in place of the separate feet that were so extensively used later, and a dial which had separate small dials for seconds at six o'clock and alarm-setting at twelve. The press-on back was perforated for winding-keys, hand- and alarm-setting and regulation. A feature that has not been perpetuated is a small loop at the back to hang the clock on a nail if desired. As this loop was fastened to the removable back rather than the drum case, a certain element of danger was present. To clear the handsetters and winding-keys when the clock was hung on the wall, the back was deeply dished. Such a clock as this might rouse little excitement if it were discovered in a box of junk, but it is a most important historical document and has provided the inspiration for many similar clocks down the years.

The Seth Thomas alarm was $4\frac{1}{4}$ inches in diameter on the back plate with a 3-inch dial, and a similar model with time only was produced. This did not have the subsidiary dial for alarm-setting, and the bell was naturally absent, but no carrying-loop was provided. The small loop for hanging the clock on the wall was, however, still included. The name of the model was 'Nutmeg', possibly a humorous reference to the time when Yankee pedlars were selling wooden nutmegs to unsuspecting customers.

As the Ingraham business was founded on making wooden cases, it would not be expected that they would have been early in the field with metal-cased clocks. The catalogue of 1880 does not contain any of this type, although lever clocks in wooden cases are present. The New Haven catalogue for the same year, however, contains a number of the type and also includes alarms and timepieces with day of the month indication outside the main figures. By 1889 the range had greatly increased, and similar movements were being offered in a number of novelty cases. An important development was the making of a clock about half the size of a normal alarm which would today be known as a '2-inch' and which has been very popular with many manufacturers in both America and Germany. The name of the New Haven model is 'Sting', and one variation of it includes normal hour-striking with facility of repeat up to ten minutes before striking the next hour. This model is priced at only $4.60, when the alarm version costs $3.25. The basic movement has screw pillars and polished steel pinions, a straight line-lever with double roller, club-tooth escapement and polished springs. The same movement is also put up in the form of a pocket watch.

Not only New Haven had begun to miniaturize their production: Waterbury also had been working on the problem and in 1892 were approached by Robert H. Ingersoll to manufacture a pocket watch based on their smallest drum clock, which had a dial about 2 inches in diameter. The order was accepted for twelve thousand pieces under the condition that they were all taken within a year. The watches were sold, although not without some difficulty, and the business continued to expand. The watches were much thicker than the normal pocket watch at the time but could be easily carried by a farm labourer in his trousers pocket. The back of the case had to be opened for winding and setting the hands, and there was really very little difference from the miniature drum clock on which the design was based except that the pendant was more like that of a normal watch. By the early years of the new century, the design was obsolete in its form of a watch, for new models had been developed more on the lines of the traditional watch.

Among the clock firms that produced these newly developed models were Ansonia and New Haven. Their product had a nickel case with stem-winding and setting and both possessed seconds-hands. The Western Clock Manufacturing Company also produced a watch at this time. It was slightly larger than the others, being size 18 as against the Ansonia and New Haven size 16, and while it had stem winding, it was set from the back.

It was not a novelty for firms that made clocks to go in for watch-production. Edward Howard of Boston had taken up watch-manufacture in the 1850s, and the Seth Thomas Company had begun production in 1884 after building a special shop for the work. Both these undertakings were, however, based on the traditional watch rather than the miniaturization of existing designs of drum clock. It would add to the interest of a collection of American clocks to include one or more watches by the well known clock-factories.

E. N. Welch and Waterbury were both supplying drum clocks during the 1880s, and it seems that timepieces were as popular as alarms. Day of the month is an important feature, and possibly most production at the time was carried out under the threat of competition from the other factories. No one dared to be left out of the race. Novelties, such as a clock incorporated with an inkstand, are

A small Waterbury clock cased to be used as a watch. Left: With the dial removed.
Right: The rear side.

plentiful, and there are also clocks on struts such as were made by
Thomas Cole for the more expensive market in Britain during the
earlier part of the century. Ansonia in 1886 were offering models
with twenty-four-hour dial and had begun to decorate dials in
colour, a fashion which is still with us today.

By 1889 New Haven had not only put a selection of coloured dials
on the market but was also offering automata. The pallet-arbor was
arranged to project through the dial and, as it vibrated, would give

the effect of a man shaving, a girl playing a lute, another powdering her face and even a bull fight. This feature has been popular for many years, and large numbers of clocks involving moving Disney characters were made during the 1930s and after. A variation of the theme was to have the scapewheel-arbor prolonged and the movement show the wheel of a paddle steamer rotating or the sails of a windmill. The idea was an old one, having been used extensively on the dials of long-case clocks in Holland during the eighteenth century and also to a limited extent in Britain. It was also known on the less expensive clocks from the Black Forest. The extra mechanism is something extra to go wrong, and therefore the clock stands a chance of being laid aside earlier than a standard model, hence the comparative rarity of older specimens today. These clocks form items for specialist collectors in America. A simpler version of the idea is to have a well-known character in the centre of the dial, whose arms are formed by the hands.

By 1904 the number of models offered by the various factories had greatly increased. Ingraham had now entered the field with a drum-alarm that looks more modern than most of the other models, and novelty clocks abound. The 2-inch-dial clocks were now being put into marble cases, and many more were being supplied with porcelain cases that are still seen at antique markets. The miniature clock was also being made to run for eight days and was supplied with alarm in some of the thirty-hour models. A particularly well-known clock of the small type was the 'Bee' made by Ansonia, which was mentioned in a Bulldog Drummond story. In the 1886 catalogue this clock had been advertised as having solid-cut pinions and winding without a (separate) key. Perhaps the most significant items were the products of the Parker Clock Company of Meriden, Connecticut. These clocks all employed a concentric hand for setting the alarm, but the most important feature of the design was that the bell had been removed from the top of the case and placed inside. This feature has become so universally accepted that in recent years reproduction alarm-clocks have been made with the bell on top again, just to be different.

The Waterbury catalogue for 1908 also contains a large number of novelty clocks with its quota of Art Nouveau cases. From 1880 to 1910 it seems that the balance clock was gaining an ever stronger hold on the market, but where have all these clocks disappeared to? The probable answer is that they were taken to repairers who did not

One-day Cottage Striking clock by Waterbury Clock Co., and Sharp Gothic
alarm by Ansonia Brass and Copper Co., 1869-78

Sharp Gothics by Jerome, *(left)* thirty-hour striking and *(right)* timepiece, both *c.* 1880

Thirty-hour Beehive by E. N. Welch

consider them worth the trouble of repairing and recommended a replacement. In view of the number of different styles offered, it seems reasonable to assume that some of them at least must have escaped and now be waiting in attics, garden sheds or obscure cupboards to be retrieved and treated as collectors' items. Virtually any old alarm-clock with the name of one of the famous American factories on it is a collectors' item, but it is only recently that anyone in the USA has begun to specialize in the type. Collectors in Britain have less opportunity of finding them as so many alarm-clocks sold there were from German factories.

Before leaving the subject of alarm-clocks and small 2-inch clocks, mention should be made of the Western Clock Manufacturing Company, which has already come into the story in connection with pocket watches. This firm had its beginnings in 1888 and was located at La Salle, Illinois, far removed from the main centres of Connecticut. The firm specialized in balance clocks and in its catalogue for 1902 was advertising a selection of alarm-clocks of the conventional type and 2-inch movements in a variety of cases, some of which were of metal but others were imported and made of porcelain. The normal alarm-clock sold for 53 cents trade and a slightly superior model at 54 cents. An alarm which would ring for two minutes could be supplied for 58 cents. The basic 2-inch clock in a drum case could be supplied for 50 cents in a tin box and 49 cents in a paper box. The alarm models all have the bell on top, and none of them shows seconds.

This firm became famous in later years for such models as the 'Big Ben', introduced in 1910, and the 'Baby Ben', introduced in 1915. A speciality of the Western Clock Manufacturing Company was to make lantern-pinions by mounting the wires in molten metal of a low fusing-point, which economized on brass and speeded up manufacture. The name was later changed to 'Western Clock Company' and finally 'Westclox' which was formerly a trademark.

The wheels from a Westclox movement, showing the method of embedding pinion wires in molten metal.

The firm still exists as part of the General Time Corporation. A later development of the Parker models incorporated in Westclox products was that the back of the case formed the bell, thereby saving space and also metal. The switch for silencing the alarm and that for determining whether the alarm sounded in one continuous peal or intermittently were placed on the top of the case roughly between ten and two.

There are two important styles of balance clock that have not been dealt with so far. The carriage clock was mentioned earlier, and in view of its popularity in Europe, it is not surprising that it was imitated by American factories. The earliest reference to American carriage clocks is found in the Ansonia catalogue for 1880. The escapement was mounted on a platform even though it was a pin pallet, but it was placed parallel to the dial instead of in the usual fore-and-aft position. Six models were shown, and three of them bore the patent date of 1877. This was before the company had moved to Brooklyn and when it was still operating from Ansonia, Connecticut. Two of the models appear to be eight-day clocks, three of them have alarm and one has strike and repeat. One of the alarms has a curved glass which is also found occasionally on French models.

The next example traced in a catalogue is by Waterbury in 1881. There is only one model which is named 'Traveler' (*sic*), and the finish of the case is nickel, while the clock can be supplied with alarm if desired. The appearance is very like that of the French carriage clock of the period except that the company's trademark appears on the lower part of the dial. By 1885 E. N. Welch had brought out two models, one with strike, repeat and alarm, and the other with time and alarm or time and strike. These clocks together with the Waterbury 'Traveler' ran only one day on a winding.

As time went on, more models with eight-day movements were made, and a selection of leather travelling-cases was offered to assist when the clocks were being transported. While an American carriage clock looks very much the same as a French one from the front, an inspection of the movement will usually give away its origin.

The other balance clock that should be mentioned is a clock that resembles the carriage clock in outline but which is somewhat larger and has a case made of tinplate instead of brass. As in the carriage clock, the sides are glass panels. The movement corresponds with that of the normal size of alarm-clock. The design made its debut in

The Seth Thomas 'Joker'. Left: Post 1879. Right: A variation, the 'Student', *c.* 1904.

the Seth Thomas catalogue of 1879 under the name of 'Joker Lever' and was also made by other firms under different names. To all intents and purposes it was the drum-alarm adapted to a rectangular case with the bell hidden below. These clocks must have been popular, for they are still seen today, although not necessarily in the original Seth Thomas version.

The disadvantage of collecting balance-controlled clocks is that repairs are sometimes difficult, especially if the scapewheel teeth are worn. While many of the pendulum movements can still be provided with parts from material-dealers, it is more of a problem with balance clocks, especially where the small sizes are concerned. New 2-inch movements are on the market, but if an old movement is replaced by a new one, it is only the case of the clock that is being preserved. It is an encouraging thought, though, that this branch of collecting is still new and that there is plenty of scope for research from both the historical and the technical standpoint.

6 Off the Beaten Track

The evolution of the American clock has been traced as a reasonably continuous narrative culminating in the production of thousands of clocks per annum by a limited number of very large undertakings. In addition to the main story there were numerous attempts to design and produce clocks that form an interesting sideline, and the products are, of course, collectors' items in their own right.

When the very early days of clockmaking in America are considered, when metal was scarce and equipment was often of a very primitive kind, it would be expected that some unconventional clocks would be produced. A number of early long-case clocks are known showing where unusual methods have been followed because of difficult circumstances, but anything dating from the pre-factory era is difficult to acquire today on account of high prices and also because most of the available specimens have remained in their own country. The early factory clocks made of wood were also not a regular export-item, and consequently these are also difficult to come by. As early as this period, however, departures from normal production were taking place as people tried to overcome the Terry patent, and unusual clocks were produced in quantity rather than as one-off jobs.

Silas Hoadley, Terry's former partner, produced his own version of the shelf-clock movement which more or less turned the Terry design literally upside-down. As the cords for the weights passed over pulleys at the top of the case, it was no disadvantage to have the barrels at the top of the movement, and as the great wheel of the striking-train carried the pins for actuating the hammer, the hammer and bell were also placed above. Unlike the Terry clock, the escapement was between the plates, and the crutch pointed upwards. The motion-work was inside, as on the Terry design, and the clocks were sometimes sold under the name of 'Franklin Clocks', Benjamin Franklin's saying 'Time is Money' being printed on the label. The appearance of the clock was that of a normal Pillar-and-Scroll type, but the type of movement was given away by the position of the winding-holes which came near ten and two instead of near eight and four. Hoadley's design was on the market roughly between 1826 and 1829 when the Pillar and Scroll was going out of favour.

Two 'Swingers' from Ansonia's 1880 catalogue.

A small Gilbert alarm. Left: Apparently no unusual features. Right: The arrangement on S. B. Terry's principle with the escapement between the plates.

The North family of Torrington, Connecticut, produced another variation of the Terry movement, but here the plates were made very long and the movement was arranged horizontally with the weights descending straight below the barrels instead of having the cords carried over pulleys. The Torrington movement had the escapement on the front plate, as in Terry's arrangement, and was often housed in the normal Pillar-and-Scroll case. A Torrington clock gives itself away by having the winding-holes opposite nine and three and being very wide apart.

Noble and Chauncey Jerome were in business together in the 1820s, and they used a movement differing from the Terry type which had been designed for them by Chauncey Boardman and is nicknamed a 'Groaner' on account of the noise it makes when striking. This movement had the motion-work on the front plate and driven from a wheel mounted on the arbor of the main wheel, as in the old wooden hang-up clocks, and the escapement was between the plates.

Joseph Ives has already been mentioned as introducing various new features into clock-movements during the early-nineteenth century. He is known for his wagon-springs and particularly for rolling-pinions where the shrouds of the lantern-pinions are made to rotate in order to reduce friction. A disadvantage is that the lantern-pinions have to be larger and are more difficult to make. Ives's early clocks had wheels with square-ended teeth which did not give good gearing even with rolling-pinions, and he later had to re-design his movements. He used iron in his movements quite extensively. The idea of roller-pinions was not new, having been used by John Harrison in the early-eighteenth century.

The firm of Ingrahams used steel plates in some of their movements. This lasted for only a few years at the beginning of the present century but was found to be unsatisfactory and was soon discontinued. The trouble arose because the steel pivots wore the holes in the steel plates. Other makers used steel plates but would insert brass bushes. An Ingraham clock with steel plates is therefore a rarity and a collectors' piece. It may be found that the steel plates have been brassed over for the sake of appearance. This idea suggests the Charles Kirke movement with a cast-iron back-plate incorporating guards for the mainsprings produced some sixty years earlier.

The Howard catalogue for 1874 includes a number of clocks with marble dials. These were intended for large rooms such as those of hotels, halls or banks, and the advantage claimed was that they were easy to keep clean as they had no glass, and the marble surface could be wiped over. There cannot be many of them left now, as the material is fragile and so many large buildings have been torn down in the last century. It is unlikely that any interest would have been shown in these clocks or attempts made to preserve them until very recent years when interest in clocks has become more widespread.

The balance-movement and cases made of iron were both known by the 1850s. During the 1870s clocks were made in the form of human figures or animals in cast iron and were fitted with balance-movements that caused the figure to blink its eyes as the clock ran. This idea had already been used in the Black Forest, but with pendulum movements, and had enjoyed a revival during the 1850s and 1860s. The American examples are occasionally seen in Britain, but the mortality rate on all balance-controlled clocks has been high.

THE CALENDAR CLOCK

There was one variation of the normal clock that was really popular with many different factories and with several different types of mechanism. This was the calendar clock. Mention has already been made of some clocks, usually with 12-inch dials, that showed the date, but sometimes clocks of the drum type, with or without alarm, had the day of the month indicated outside the main figures. These do not really come into the category of calendar clocks for the short months would need adjusting by hand, as would Leap Year. Several inventors designed calendar mechanisms that would deal with these matters automatically, and they arranged for the larger clock-factories to produce the clocks which incorporated their device.

The calendar clock proper usually has a separate dial for the calendar information and does not indicate the days outside the hour-figures. The Ithaca Calendar Clock Company of Ithaca, New York, existed from 1865 to 1914, and the system of indicating the date was to use a dial about the same size as the normal dial of the clock with thirty-one days marked on its circumference, while two horizontal windows in the centre showed the name of the day and the month. The mechanism was patented by H. B. Horton, who was granted several patents on calendar mechanism. The company produced calendar clocks in many different styles.

The Seth Thomas Company began making calendar clocks in 1862, based on patents belonging to Huntington & Platts of Ithaca, New York. These patents incorporated older ones, the earliest of which was by J. H. Hawes, but it did not allow for Leap Year. In 1876 the Company changed to a mechanism patented by Randall T. Andrews, who was a relative of the founder, and this mechanism was used until the Company ceased producing calendar clocks in 1917. By 1888 there were fifteen different models being offered. The layout of the dial was the same as that described for the Ithaca clock above.

Benjamin B. Lewis was granted a patent in 1862 whereby the month and the day were shown by concentric hands on a dial below the main one, and the rights of manufacture were sold to E. Burwell of Bristol, Connecticut. In 1864 the indication of the name of the day on the main dial was patented, and in 1868 a third patent improved the reliability of the mechanism. In 1867 Lewis began manufacturing for himself. A feature of one of these clocks is the instruction

A Seth Thomas calendar clock with (right) the mechanism showing.

carried on the paper not to open the door between 8 pm and 8 am, as the bar which moved the calendar was in the way of the pin between those hours. In 1870 Welch, Spring & Co obtained exclusive rights to manufacture Lewis's mechanism and fitted it to a number of wall clocks and two shelf clocks. After the Welch, Spring Company was dissolved, Lewis manufactured his mechanism for a year in the same factory, but it was burned down in 1885, and thereafter manufacture ceased. Lewis sold his mechanisms to E. Ingraham & Co of

A pair of small timepieces by E. N. Welch, made in the 1870s. Above: Note that the dial of the right hand is a replacement. Below: The left of the Welch movements has B. B. Lewis's special escapement; that on the right is a normal Welch with typical solid scapewheel.

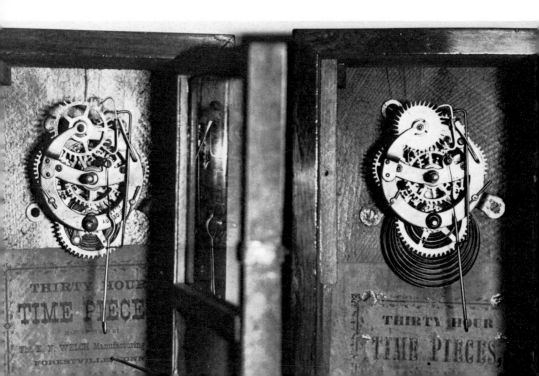

Bristol, and Jerome & Co of New Haven (New Haven Clock Company).

Daniel J. Gale of Sheboygan, Wisconsin, received a patent for a calendar mechanism in 1869 and another in 1871. He then went to work for Welch, Spring & Co. The Company produced clocks under his patents, the first being circular-dial clocks with dials 24 inches, 18 inches and 12 inches in diameter. Gale's system used the edge of the dial to carry the numbers for the days of the month, which was indicated by a long single hand corresponding to the minute-hand on a normal clock. Between the centre and top of the dial was a subsidiary dial for indicating hours and minutes in the normal way. In the corresponding position below the centre of the dial was another dial to indicate the month, and at the three o'clock and nine o'clock positions were smaller dials to indicate the day of the week and the phases of the moon. The latter were shown by a hand rotating over a dial in the usual manner, with new moon and full moon at the top and bottom and a half moon at the corresponding quarters. There was no disc partially obscured as used on long-case clocks for showing the phase of the moon.

Welch, Spring & Co controlled two important patents for calendar

Two versions of the Gale calendar clock from Welch's 1880 catalogue.

clocks, but with the winding-up of the Company in 1884 and the subsequent period of difficulty for E. N. Welch, production was able to take place over only a limited period. The Southern Calendar Clock Company of St Louis was also a firm that did not have a long life. It began business in 1875 and used movements supplied by Seth Thomas. Sales were direct to customers with easy terms possible if the cash were not available. The business closed in 1889, but operations were revived for a short time in the nineties. The clocks are distinguished by the word 'Fashion' on the glass. The firm was really a sales organization which sent out a group of salesmen to a district where they would hire accommodation, move in a supply of clocks and then go out selling from door to door. When all possible business had been completed, the operation was repeated in the next town. A book of 'Instructions' was given with each clock, but it contained no instructions at all, only jokes, proverbs and advertisements for the clocks. Most of these books have been destroyed, but if a clock is acquired with its accompanying book, it will greatly add to the interest.

Another firm in the calendar clock business was the Prentiss Calendar and Time Company of New York, which was sold in 1892. This firm produced a model in which day, month and date were shown in large windows, but the calendar-mechanism had to be wound separately from the time-mechanism. The Maranville Calendar mechanism had the thirty-one figures for the days of the month outside the hour-figures as on many other designs, but next to each figure was a window which allowed the name of the day to show through, and this changed at the end of the month. The name of the month appeared in an extra window at the top of the dial.

American clock-production was aimed mainly at the cheaper market, but a limited amount of higher-class work was done during the factory era. Edward Howard of Boston was early in the field and his versions of the Banjo clock and the marble-dial clocks for public rooms have already been mentioned. Welch, Spring & Co intended from the beginning to produce work of a higher quality than was being turned out by the E. N. Welch factory, and in addition to the spring-driven clocks already mentioned, they made weight-driven wall clocks with dead-beat escapements and either centre-seconds or seconds indicated on a subsidiary dial. The plates were solid, but lantern-pinions were used. These clocks were designed by B. B. Lewis, who produced the calendar-mechanism sold by the firm.

The famous Seth Thomas
No 2 Regulator from the 1863 catalogue.

Many of the calendar clocks were made on the lines of domestic 'Regulators' and, in spite of the solid plates, did not always have dead-beat escapements.

The Seth Thomas catalogue for 1863 contained a model known as 'the number 2 Regulator' which was simply a circular dial with a trunk below, the whole clock being 34 inches high. It ran for eight days and was weight-driven with the winding-hole in the two o'clock position. This clock must hold a record, for it continued to be offered until 1950, a period of nearly ninety years. Later examples include a subsidiary dial to show seconds. (An example of this clock would be well worth adding to a collection.) Not only Seth Thomas but also other factories produced clocks of this type. Gilbert advertised them in 1875, Waterbury in 1881, but New Haven first included them in the catalogue for 1889, although spring-driven equivalents had been offered earlier in the decade.

The American version of the Vienna Regulator with spring-drive has already been mentioned, but various firms also brought out a weight-driven model. The Gilbert models of 1875 do not greatly resemble the prototype; neither do the Waterbury offerings of 1881, where the weights are hanging near the edge of the case, but Seth Thomas in 1879 is offering a model entitled 'Regulator No 4' which comes much closer. There is a polished veneered back to the case to set off the pendulum, and the top of the glass is curved. The Ansonia catalogue of 1886 shows two models named 'Mecca' and 'Medina' which also resemble the product of the German factories at the time. The St Louis Clock and Silverware catalogue of 1904 and the Waterbury of 1908 both include weight-driven clocks which owe something to the Vienna Regulator, but there is no attempt to reproduce Continental designs. The Waterbury models still have the weights towards the side of the case, which, although theoretically correct, is unhappy from an artistic point of view. American weight-driven wall clocks based on the Vienna type are extremely rare in Britain, and it can only be concluded that the German factories were monopolizing the British market at the time. A Birmingham wholesaler's catalogue published about 1890 shows fifty-two designs of Vienna Regulator cases and offers each with a timepiece or strike movement, making 104 variations. All these clocks were supplied by only one German factory.

It may come as a surprise that the Waterbury Company was offering four different models of the type we now know as a 'Berliner' or 'Freeswinger'. This clock has a solid wooden case with circular dial enclosed by a bezel and stands on a bracket which is integral with the case and has an exposed pendulum below. This type is extremely rare in Britain and was made by German factories chiefly for the home market.

INVENTORS AND THEIR PATENTS

Numerous inventors were granted patents for improvements to clock-mechanisms in the USA, and many clocks bear the word 'Patented' together with a date. This may refer to some special feature of the mechanism or even be the design of the case. A book was published in 1949 by George H. Eckhard listing and classifying American horological patents, and a copy is to be found in the British Library (formerly Patent Office Library) near Chancery Lane, London. In the Chancery Lane Safe Deposit Building almost adjacent are kept specifications of overseas patents, including those from America. A great deal can be learned from these records.

Patent records are not the only place to discover horological inventions. Old periodicals and encyclopedias often contain information that suggests new features to be looked for when searching for clocks. It is never certain that a clock has been made incorporating the new feature, but it always pays to be on the alert. An idea of this type was printed in the *Scientific American* for 1846. It was an invention by John S. Grieg and was intended to overcome the difficulty of having to set a pendulum clock to the correct level. An iron plate shaped like a pendulum was suspended from the same centre as the scapewheel and was free to move so that it always took up a vertical position. The split stud from which the pendulum suspension was hung was fastened a little way below the pallets into the iron plate, and the stud on which the pallets rode was also fixed to the plate. The theory was that, as the iron piece always took up a vertical position and the pendulum and pallets were supported by it, the clock would automatically be in beat whatever the level of the shelf on which it stood. In practice, the swinging of the pendulum would probably have set the iron piece swinging too and eventually have cancelled out all the motion. So far no clock has been seen with this device, but quite possibly a prototype existed at one time and may still be lying in some forgotten spot.

One inventor in particular who is worthy of mention is Florence Kroeber. He was born in Cologne, Germany, in 1840, went to America with his parents in 1850 and entered the clock business in 1859, becoming his own master in 1863. He imported clocks from Europe, rather a strange activity in view of the tremendous production then going on in Connecticut, but later he began inventing and patenting various ideas of his own. One of his later labels describes him as agent for New Haven, E. N. Welch, Jerome, Seth Thomas and other Companies. The address is 10 Cortlandt Street, New York, and the advice is given 'Send for catalogue'. So far a Kroeber catalogue has not been located, but no doubt it would contain an interesting selection of what the principal factories were offering.

Kroeber began patenting his ideas in 1869 with designs for clock-cases. In 1874 he produced a method of releasing the striking-work of a clock that allowed the hands to be turned backwards, and it is substantially the method found on many German clocks made in the nineteenth and twentieth centuries. A small hook raises a trip-lever which in its turn raises the strike-release wire. The movement

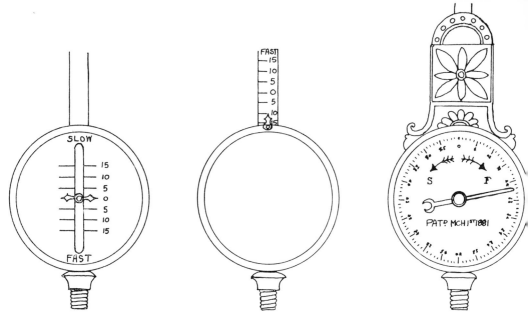

Three variations of the Kroeber pendulum. Other firms, such as Ansonia and Welch, produced their own versions of the idea.

illustrated possesses the double-slotted cam that was used on the Ansonia movement with pins for raising the hammer. As the Ansonia movement was not patented until later in the decade, this movement may be that of some other factory, possibly E. N. Welch, but the interesting point is that this method of striking was already established by 1874. In the same year Kroeber patented some case-designs which must be very early Walnuts, and then he produced another version of the strike-release mechanism. In 1876 a clock-case resembling Ingraham's Venetian was provided with a sliding door made of glass to protect the pendulum-bob. The aim was to give the bob as much space as possible, and this was achieved by using a piece of glass that would be thinner than a piece of wood of equivalent strength. In the same year came a new version of the escapement that allows a doll to swing to and fro below the clock and act as a pendulum. Clocks with this type of mechanism are generally French. More cases and a novelty alarm-clock follow, but the best known of Kroeber's inventions was his recording pendulum. The first presentation of this idea was to have a vertical slot in the centre of the bob, and a pointer was fixed to the rod of the pendulum and projected through this slot. The middle of the slot was marked zero, and a scale of minutes was marked above and below the zero-mark. When the clock was started, the bob was put at zero and ran for twenty-four hours, after which the error was noted and the bob was moved up or down by the number of minutes shown on the scale. After this, the clock theoretically kept time. If desired, a glass could be put over the bob and pointer.

Some clocks have been seen with this type of pendulum, but so far it has not been traced in a manufacturer's catalogue. A later development of the idea, however, appears in the catalogues of Welch for 1885, Ansonia for 1886 and New Haven for 1889. In this version the pendulum-bob was formed into a dial with a pointer, and numbers indicating minutes were marked on each side of the zero-point, which was at the top. Behind the bob the pendulum-rod was formed into a stirrup to clear the arbor of the pointer, and a piece of cord was fastened to the top and bottom of the stirrup by wax with one turn passing round the arbor. The theory was that, as the bob was raised or lowered, the cord would pull the indicator round to show the number of minutes by which the clock would lose or gain as a result of the operation. The accuracy of the reading leaves room for doubt.

Kroeber was not the only inventor whose patents are seen on clocks. H. J. Davies was another whose name crops up, and there are many more whose work would be of interest if it were documented. There is a wide field here for historical research.

Some inventors produced clocks that were completely separated from the normal development of design, and among the early ones was Aaron D. Crane of Caldwell, New Jersey, and Newark, New Jersey. Crane obtained his first patent in 1829, but as all American patent records were destroyed in 1836, it is not known what this was for. His next was obtained in 1841 and was for a clock going for a year controlled by a torsion pendulum. In 1845 a small factory was organized to manufacture this clock, but it was not a great success, and the business failed. The clock was being produced at a time when there was still a mainspring problem, and it was a delicate mechanism, unlike those that were to sweep the market in the next decade. Crane's first design had a single spherical weight at the bottom of the pendulum, but a further patent in 1855 provided for two or more weights. His aim in designing the clock was to involve the minimum amount of friction, and hence he used the lightest possible driving-weights. He also designed turret clocks on the torsion-pendulum principle. Aaron D. Crane died in 1860, but his clocks had not been a success up to that time as they were too much of a quality product to

A Briggs rotary-pendulum clock from the E. N. Welch Company, 1870s.

New Haven's 'Clyde', a 'Walnut' with a Kroeber pendulum.

capture the market. The principle of the torsion pendulum with a long period of running became popular after about 1880, but it was mainly German factories that made the type, and the principle found little application in America. S. B. Terry had patented a torsion movement in 1852, but no developments seem to have been made to it.

John C. Briggs of Concord, New Hampshire, patented a clock with a rotary pendulum in 1855/6, and a number of these were made by E. N. Welch in the 1870s. The clock was kept under a glass shade, and the tiny pendulum rotated in front of the dial. The idea had first been suggested by Jost Bodeker in 1587 for the clock of the cathedral at Osnabruck, and later, in 1673, Christiaan Huygens, the Dutch mathematician, described a method for arranging an accurate rotary pendulum by making the bob follow a parabolic path if it changed its height for any reason. It is doubtful whether Briggs knew about these ideas, but as he was a civil engineer, he might have got his inspiration from the governor of a steam-engine. His pendulum simply consisted of a ball suspended from a cord with no compensation, and the clocks performed well enough for ordinary domestic duties. The number made was not large. A notable feature of the Briggs clock was the multi-armed winding-key below, often called 'The Spider'.

A clock of a different kind based on rotary motion was the 'Ignatz' or flying-pendulum clock. This was patented by A. C. Clausen in 1883 and put into production during the latter part of 1884 by New Haven, using the Jerome name. It was offered in three styles of case, oak, mahogany and ebony, and in the following year four styles were offered, but it was discontinued after that year because of its inability to keep time.

The clock case was surmounted by a horizontal swinging arm from the outer end of which a small ball was hanging on a thread. The mechanism of the clock tended to rotate the arm, but as it did so, the ball swung outwards and was interrupted at each side of the clock by the thread catching on a vertical post. The momentum caused the thread to wrap itself round the post and immediately unwind again. Another wire above prevented the thread from going further until it had wound itself round the post again in the opposite direction. After it unwound the second time, the arm would carry the ball to the opposite side of the clock, and the process would be repeated. The clocks were notoriously inaccurate in spite of the Company's advertisement to the contrary, and it is not surprising that they did not become popular. They were useful as a shop-window attraction.

Another idea that was unconventional but which had a longer life was the 'Swinger'. Here the clock and pendulum form one unit which in effect is a double pendulum and therefore swings more slowly than a normal pendulum of the same size. The pendulum is usually supported on the outstretched hand of a statuette. The movement is about the size of a pocket-watch and has a weight inside working on the principle of the pedometer.

The design first appears in the Ansonia Catalogue for 1880, where three models of the usual type were offered and in addition there was a wall version suspended in front of a mirror. By 1886 the mirror version had disappeared, and the one with figures of a hunter and a falconer supporting the swinging clock between them had been altered to two female figures in classical costume which corresponded to the single-figure models. The type is well known in

Britain, but so far an American example has not been encountered. All clocks seen have been German.

The 'Plato' clock was an early example of a digital clock but was mechanical instead of electric. The shape was that of a carriage-clock, and hours and minutes were each indicated by a separate pack of cards which was slowly rotated by the clock-mechanism. A finger held a card back to show the time, and after the card had been displayed for the correct interval, it slipped away from the finger, and the next one took its place.

It was patented by Eugene L. Fitch in 1902 and was made in four models by Ansonia, 1904–6. The movement was contained in the base which was somewhat deeper than that of a normal carriage clock.

The Yale Clock Company of New Haven, Connecticut, produced some tiny clocks which would normally have been provided with balances but were made as a novelty with tiny visible pendulums. The cases were of metal, but the shape was like that of the 'Cottage' design produced by a number of the large factories.

The World's Fair at Chicago in 1893 was held to commemorate the four-hundredth anniversary of the voyage of Columbus. (Adverse circumstances caused it to be held a year late.) A novelty offered at the fair was a wooden clock controlled by a foliot very similar to the reproductions of the earliest type of clock made in the Black Forest. The dial bears a portrait of Columbus and the date 1492, which is sometimes accepted as the date of the clock. These clocks were made by the Bostwick & Burgess Manufacturing Company of Norwalk, Ohio, and about twenty thousand examples were produced. The price at first was $5 but at the end was reduced to $1. They were not accurate timekeepers and were nothing more than a novelty.

In complete contrast to the Columbus clock was a horological product made from 1941 in Pennsylvania. This was the range of marine chronometers produced by the Hamilton Watch Company of Lancaster, Pennsylvania, at the request of the US Government, on account of the difficulty of obtaining them from Europe. The firm had already produced marine chronometers in 1918, but production came so late in the war that a number were left on the makers' hands and were disposed of privately in subsequent years. Development of the new models was begun in 1940, and production began in 1941, reaching its peak in 1944. Total production was about eleven

A Waterbury
alarm with the
winding-hole at
XI. The alarm
mechanism is in a
separate frame,
well below the
main movement.

thousand pieces. Hamilton chronometers are now becoming
collectors' items.

Another facet of clock-production in America was the use of clocks
for advertisement purposes. Among the pioneers was Edward P.
Baird who began in Montreal and later moved to Plattsburgh, New
York. His first type of clock was vaguely reminiscent of the
Ingraham Ionic, but round the dial and over the door were placed
rings of *papier mâché* which had been embossed with advertising

slogans. The movements of the clocks were by Seth Thomas, as Baird was a friend of the Thomas family. Among products to be advertised by Baird clocks was Coca Cola, and the clocks were offered to dealers who sold more than 100 gallons per year. The clocks were even seen in Britain. One favourite slogan seen on grocers' shop clocks was 'Milkmaid Milk. Now's the time to buy it', and another product advertised was Vanner and Prest's 'Molliscorium', a preparation for keeping leather supple. Tobacco was another commodity which was advertised by Baird clocks. A small book has been written on the activities of Baird, and it also demonstrates that there is still a lot of work to be done in connection with research on his activities.

Another field for research is clocks that just fail to meet the required standard of excellence. For instance, a charming little Sharp Gothic alarm by Waterbury had the alarm-movement as a separate unit in the bottom of the case. The winding-hole for the time-train, however, was at eleven o'clock, and if one retired at that hour the clock could not be wound, as the hand covered the winding-hole. Another small movement by Ansonia had the plates fastened together by nuts, but the pillar under the scapewheel was so masked by the latter that it was very difficult to screw the nut on and to remove it. One wonders why this sort of thing was not spotted earlier and the design modified before production began.

It has been possible to deal with only a limited number of unusual items in American horological history. Numerous patents have been issued, but in many cases it is not known whether the idea was actually put into production. The collector of American clocks, therefore, always stands a chance of finding something that has been forgotten for generations, and this is one of the most attractive features of the subject. Even slight variations in the design of normal models make a clock interesting to a collector, so it is worthwhile to study as many clocks as possible in order to find out what are the normal features of the products of the various firms.

7 Imitations and Reproductions

Whenever anyone has a successful idea, it is not long before other people are trying to imitate him. When Eli Terry started making clocks by mass production and it proved a success, many imitators were soon in the field, and as a result the Connecticut clock-industry was established on a firm basis. Later, when Jerome sent his cheap brass-movement clocks to Britain and was successful, other firms were ready to follow his example, and the number of clocks crossing the Atlantic became a flood. By 1854 the port of Liverpool was handling sixty thousand pieces annually valued at £30,000.

The OG was better than anything that had been seen on the British market before at a cheap price. All moderately priced clocks sold in Britain up to 1840 had come from the Black Forest and were wall clocks with exposed weights and pendulum. The frames were of wood, and so were the arbors, but the wheels were of brass, and the clocks were good timekeepers and gave comparatively little trouble. The exposed weights and pendulum were, however, subject to the attention of children and cats. A strong draught could set the chains swinging so that they caught the pendulum and stopped the clock. The wooden frame sagged over a long period and gradually pinched the pivots so that the wheels would not move. The clock stood out a long way from the wall, which made it vulnerable, and it was not particularly decorative. The normal Black Forest clock had a gaily painted dial, but for some reason this type of dial was not popular in Britain, where Black Forest movements were given circular dials with mahogany surrounds and brass bezels with very convex glasses.

The new American clock, with its coloured glass tablet and its mahogany veneered case, was a complete contrast. The weights were hidden, and the clock was wound by a key which was much more sophisticated than pulling a weight up by a chain. The problem of children, cats and draughts was taken care of, and the clock stood out at less distance from the wall. It could be stood on a side table or on a cupboard or be hung on the wall without having to leave an empty space below it for the weights to fall through. It was not cheap when compared with the wages of the day, but it was not so expensive as a British clock. No wonder it became popular.

GERMAN IMITATIONS

Production in the Black Forest had been rising up to 1840, with Britain as one of the best customers, but from then on it began to fall as the new American clocks captured the market. The only solution to the problem was to produce clocks in factories, as was being done in America, and give up the small workshops where the Black Forest clockmakers worked. It was also necessary to scrap old designs and produce the type of clock that was being made in America. The pioneer in Germany was Erhard Junghans of Schramberg, and he began by making clock accessories only and produced complete clocks later. It is believed that the first type he made was the 'Marine or Locomotive' with the octagonal wooden surround, but so far no specimen has come to light, although a clock of this type has been seen that could very well have been an early Junghans product.

The OG was the most popular American design, and Junghans produced his own version of it. It was in the manufacture of spring clocks, though, that the German imitation of American designs is most noticeable. Several other OG designs from the Black Forest have been seen, but the workmanship is far superior to that of the American ones. The cases show a standard of craftsmanship that belongs to the small workshop rather than the factory, and it is only the Junghans OGs that are a close copy of the prototype. They carry a paper printed in English that is a copy of the paper used by Jerome, and includes instructions for setting the clock running and keeping it in order. The maker of the clock is 'Junghans Brothers', but no town is mentioned. The idea is to suggest to the customer that the clock is of American manufacture.

On some German clocks the OG moulding is made double, or the design is varied in some way. In the Clock Museum at Furtwangen is a splendid specimen with a high-quality case and tablet and also a movement of the traditional type made with much thicker brass plates than the usual American example. Eight-day movements for German OG clocks are also more solid, and instead of the pallets being made of strip steel, they are solid pieces of metal as are found in mantel-clocks of higher quality.

Another feature that distinguishes American from German clocks is the placing of the gong. The American method is to have the gong-base low, and the wire gong goes upwards from the centre point. German clocks have the gong-base high, and the wire points downwards.

A 'Marine' type, probably by
Junghans, Schramberg.

An OG by Junghans. Left: Its
case is typically American.
Right: The case opened to show
the paper.

Many other German manufacturers used a paper in the case, as did the American factories, but very rarely do instructions appear. Trademarks are prominent after 1875, and sometimes the word 'Schutzmarke' (trademark) gives away the clock's origin. The firms used English names, such as 'Teutonia Clock Manufactory', and did everything they could to suggest an American origin for the clocks they made, so firm was the grip of the American product on the market. Junghans issued their first catalogue in 1867, and it included various spring-driven designs that have a typically German look about them, including an example of the large spring-driven Vienna Regulator. There were two designs, however, of typically American appearance, and both have names in the American fashion. One is called 'Previosa' and resembles some of the mantel-clocks in the early Jerome catalogues, while the other is the Venetian model of Ingraham's and actually bears the same name. Both the clocks could be supplied with one-day or eight-day movements.

In 1878 the local paper published an article on the Junghans undertaking, mentioning that the factory employed three to four hundred workpeople and needed thirty horsepower from water-wheels and forty horsepower from steam-engines to operate all the machinery. The importance of the method used in the factory was to have a special machine for each process and make clocks in batches of two to five thousand. The total production for a month was about six to ten thousand pieces. Instead of polishing the cases, a special lacquer process was used which would stand up to hot climates. All clocks were issued with a guarantee for a year, and it was recommended that a clock should be cleaned every two years.

In 1876 Junghans produced their first drum-alarm clock almost simultaneously with Seth Thomas, the movement being derived from the earlier 'Marine' clocks that the firm had produced. In 1877 the first trademark was registered, an eagle surmounting a clock-dial with a banner and the words 'E Pluribus Unum'. There was still a strong suggestion of America in the publicity. In 1888 the firm registered a trademark with a five-pointed star, and in 1890 the now-familiar eight-pointed star which is still in use. By this time, however, the firm's products had developed along their own lines, and the likeness to American clocks was not so pronounced.

Junghans's greatest competitor was the Hamburg Amerikanische Uhrenfabrik, HAU in German, HAC in English. The well-known trademark of crossed arrows was introduced only in 1892, when

An American-style timepiece-movement by Philipp Haas & Söhne, St Georgen.

styles were drifting away from American models, but some of the earlier products have an American appearance, as do those of Philipp Haas & Söhne of St Georgen. This firm was the first to establish a London office, and it could be expected that more models closer to the American type would be sold by them in Britain than by other firms which came later.

It is in the realm of small cottage-timepieces and alarms that the parallel between the products of America and Germany is most apparent. There are still many of these clocks to be found in Britain, and it is often difficult to state the country of origin as so many clocks from both Germany and America have had their papers torn out. The American feature of escapement on the front plate with motion-work between plates was used, but the movements themselves do not often bear a trademark. Philipp Haas were exceptional in giving cheap movements a serial number, and one of their timepiece designs had an extremely small movement with plates more solid than usual. The firm were also exceptional in using a dead-beat escapement with pallets of the American type and in processing the plates of the movement so that they remained bright for a long time.

The origin of one of the small German timepieces can generally be determined only by noting a number of features and then striking a balance between them. Typical German characteristics are cases that are not veneered but have the finish applied to the wood of the case direct, dial-collets with very long tabs to secure them and arrows beside the winding-holes to show the direction in which the key should be turned. The door of the German clock is often secured by a brass hook like a question-mark on the outside of the case, and dials are often printed on paper stuck to the zinc backing. If a paper is present, it will probably be green, yellow or purple and have only a trademark or a model-name, without the manufacturer's name being given. Often a comparatively large case will house a very small movement. Gridiron pendulums with the letters 'R/A' on the bob will be common, but only one solitary example with 'S/F' has been seen in spite of the large sales of German clocks in Britain. The barrel-arbors in German clocks often have a brass tube surrounding them where the hook for the mainspring comes.

Having given all these German characteristics, it must be stressed that the list is not infallible. American clocks turn up with the same features, and it requires a lot of thought to decide whether a clock is German or American.

German factories do not seem to have gone in for the numerous imitations of marble clocks that the American firms produced. Walnuts were made to a limited extent, but there were no German Oaks. By the end of the nineteenth century Germany had staged a come-back on the British market, and the front pendulum-movement was giving way to the rear pendulum usually housed in wooden cases with carving as decoration, and of course the smaller versions of the spring-driven Vienna Regulator were extremely popular. Broadly speaking, it can be said that really traditional American designs were not produced in Germany after the middle 1880s.

Germany was to develop the drum-alarm and also the 2-inch movement which were competitors to the American models as the balance clock became more popular about the turn of the century. The Welch, Spring Patti timepiece had a pendulum-controlled escapement with pin-pallets and a scapewheel similar to that of a normal balance clock. The same principle has been seen applied to clocks by the Badische Uhrenfabrik of Furtwangen except that the escapement is outside the plates but at the rear. The plates themselves are in the same shape as the Patti timepiece with similar tops. The German factory has not, however, used the loop-suspension that was such a typical Black Forest feature and was used on the Patti but has applied the normal American suspension made of flattened wire. The cuckoo-clock had always been a favourite in the Black Forest and, after being turned over to factory production, was being sold in many places, even in America itself. The earliest cuckoo-clocks with metal movements had cast-brass plates, but in recent years the American type of rolled-brass plate has been employed.

Japan introduced Western methods of timekeeping after 1873, and attempts were made to establish clock-factories there, but it was not until 1886 that this was sucessfully accomplished. By this time the traditional American designs were old-fashioned, and the product for which Japan is noted is the Schoolhouse clock. Large numbers of old Japanese clocks of this type are now being imported into the USA for collectors. One such clock seen had a paper in the back of the case worded mostly in English with one or two Japanese characters and the words 'Ansonia Model'. This demonstrates the popularity of the firm's products. The movement was typical of Ansonia, and the pendulum was a mock gridiron with some leaves above the bob for decoration. Other Japanese clocks on the American pattern seen so far are mantel-clocks of c. 1900 that had wooden cases and rear pendulums that owe something to the Ansonia Tivoli and some of the products from Waterbury.

BRITISH IMPORTERS AND CASERS

Eli Terry's first venture into mass-produced clocks was for movements only. When he came to make wooden-movement shelf-clocks, his aim was to produce movement and case in one factory. In spite of this, it became a custom for certain firms to specialize in movements and for other firms to purchase these movements and fit them into their own cases. Ingraham is a good example of this, for the firm did not construct its own movements until 1865. Some of the larger factories, like Seth Thomas, not only made cases for their own movements but also sold movements for other people to case up. While most of this work was done in America, movements were also imported into Britain and cases made there. It is believed that a number of Italian workmen were employed on this task, the two favourite types of clock for this exercise being the 12-inch drop-dial and a design which has not so far been seen in an American catalogue but is found in Britain with more than one type of American movement. This is a wall clock with a smaller dial than the 12-inch type and an exposed pendulum often of the dummy mercury type with a mirror behind it, and slender turned columns beside the

case. The bottom recedes towards the wall as it descends, and the case is decorated with inlay.

One of the firms which undertook this work was Holloway & Co. William Holloway was described as 'American Merchant' in the Directory for London of the 1840s, and his advertisement says that he was agent for Jerome's American clocks since 1842. His first address was 49 Lime Street, and in 1854 he moved to 11 Tokenhouse Yard, Lothbury, disappearing from the Directory in 1856. He was one of the merchants mentioned previously who handled the importation of American clocks along with other commodities before the larger factories opened their own London offices. William Holloway's disappearance from the Directory coincides roughly with the end of Chauncey Jerome's career as an independent producer. So far the only connection with Jerome that has been established is a drop-dial with a Chauncey Jerome double-fusee movement and British-made case which bears the Holloway name. The firm of Nelson J. Holloway & Co appeared in the Directory

Opposite page: Drop-dials in English-made cases, with (left) an E. N. Welch movement and (right) a New Haven movement.

A Beehive clock from the Eagle Manufacturing Company, Portsoken, its movement having reversed fusees by Chauncey Boardman.

from 1848 onwards, and the proprietor was probably a relative of William Holloway. Importing probably led to the manufacture of cases, for the firm had more than one address, the extra building which was near to the original one probably being the workshop. The main premises were at 128/9 Minories, not far from the Tower of London, and the other building was in New Square, just behind the Minories office.

An early Beehive clock with a label of the Eagle Manufacturing Company of Portsoken has been seen. The clock has a movement by Chauncey Boardman which has reversed fusees and probably dates from 1847–50. No town called Portsoken has been traced, but the Portsoken Ward of the City of London includes the area where Holloways had their office, and this could well have been a clock that they had sold. A mantel clock with a burr-walnut case by the Eagle Manufacturing Company has also been seen but is almost certainly later. A further example in the Museum at Leicester has both the Portsoken label and the Holloway trademark, and this probably

Two Holloways. Left: The column and mirror style. Right: A large Cottage clock, with movement probably by Welch. Its tablet has a Continental atmosphere.

clinches the matter, apart from the possibility that Holloway & Co may have bought out the Eagle Manufacturing Company and sold the existing stock with their own trademark on the case.

Registration of trademarks began in Britain in 1875, and Holloway registered a crown with the letters 'H & Co'. According to the application, this trademark had been in use fifteen years, i.e. from 1861. The person registering was George Holloway, clock- and watch-manufacturer of 128 Minories. As registration took place nearly thirty years after the firm's name first appeared in the Directory, George Holloway may have been the son or nephew of Nelson J. Holloway. The firm displayed their wares at the Great Exhibition of 1862, their contribution being pendulum and lever clocks of the simplest description, and their business must have

Three German Shelf clocks.
Left Philipp Haas and Söhne;
centre and right, Junghans

OG by Junghans, grained case
not veneered and typical
Continental-style tablet

Three German Cottage clocks. That on the left Union Clock Co. Others anonymous

Miniature OG with Continental-type tablet that sugests Holloway and Co., yet the clock has an original paper of E. N. Welch

The exterior and (left) movement of a Holloway walnut-cased clock. The movement is probably by Welch.

increased over the next four years for in 1866 they opened another branch at 17 Great Alie Street, Goodman's Fields, a short distance from the Minories. This may have been for the purpose of extending the factory. Lord Grimthorpe in *Clocks, Watches and Bells* (1874) and David Glasgow in *Watch and Clock making* (1885) both comment on the practice of importing movements from America and casing them in Britain.

So far, Holloway clocks have been seen with movements by Ansonia, New Haven, Seth Thomas and E. N. Welch. A movement has also been seen like that used in the Ingraham Doric, not identical but very similar. This clock had a case generally in the shape of that model. A movement of the Welch type has also been seen in an enlarged version of the Cottage style and also in a spring-driven OG.

A later Holloway clock with (left) a very typical banded case. Its movement (right) is identical with that illustrated on the previous page, but it has a larger scapewheel for a shorter pendulum, and a bell-strike instead of a gong.

The two vertical pieces of wood which support the seatboard in a weight-driven OG are present in this example but perform no function as the movement is screwed directly to the back of the case as in a normal American spring clock. Weight-driven OGs by Holloway & Co are known, however, and the cases resemble those of Junghans in their finish. The tablets also have a Continental look and could have been painted by Italian artists in London.

The Holloway paper was brick red in colour and was more for advertisement purposes than to give instructions on the maintenance and regulation of the clock. Apparently the firm was also agent for a Swiss watch-factory called Pateck & Co, whose name resembles Patek Philippe although there was no connection.

An unusual clock has been seen with the words 'Holloway's Patent' on the dial. A typical American movement is used with an arrangement of pulleys to allow the going-train to be driven by a pair of weights while the striking-train is spring-driven as usual. The idea is to give constant power on the going side which makes for more accurate timekeeping.

New styles of Holloway case are continually being discovered, but one of their favourite types was a plain case in burr walnut with semicircular top having a Welch type of movement striking on a gong below. This is an exception to the usual rule for Holloway & Co, because practically every other model strikes on a bell. Holloway dials are quite distinctive, having hour-figures shorter than on the usual American clock, except for the OG, where the typical long, thin American figures are used.

After the reorganization of the Ansonia factory in 1878, Holloway & Co became the firm's London agents, but by 1883 the Ansonia Company had its own office at 51 Holborn Viaduct, which was then a very new thoroughfare. It seems then that the Holloway connection was dropped, for Holloway & Co disappear from the Directory altogether. They had vacated the Great Alie Street premises in 1883 and also those in New Square about the same time. It is not known whether the loss of the Ansonia representation finished the firm or whether the principals simply wanted to retire.

BRITISH IMITATIONS

The firm of Fattorini & Sons, Bradford, produced some pendulum-controlled alarm-clocks which ran for eight days and had an alarm-mechanism almost as complicated as the normal striking-work.

The Fattorini alarm, its movement shown on the right.

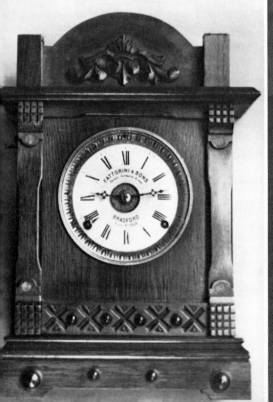

There were two hammers, one striking a gong and the other a bell, and they were placed below the movement which had plates of the lyre shape suggesting the work of Seth Thomas but which nevertheless was stamped with Fattorini's name and marked 'British Manufacture'.

The alarm was extremely noisy but could be silenced by pressing a knob at the side of the case. When the clock had run for a certain number of hours, the cancelling-button was put back to its normal position so that the alarm would sound twenty-four hours after the previous occasion. The example illustrated has the escapement and motion-work between the plates, but it is possible that there are models with a front escapement.

The movement could possibly have been made by the British United Clock Company of Birmingham, which produced a number of clocks of American type. Clocks by this firm are not very common as it lasted only about a quarter of a century (1885–1909), but during that time it built up a reputation for good work and received awards for its products at International Exhibitions. The factory produced everything required, from the tools to manufacture the clocks down to the balance-springs. Their range of work included a very small balance-movement, entitled 'Gnat' to compete with the Ansonia Bee, and pendulum-movements suitable for wall clocks with 12-inch dials. While based on American designs, the movements were of much better quality, and this may have been the reason for the firm's failure in the face of German competition.

The catalogue of the Birmingham wholesaler mentioned previously devoted a few pages to the British United Clock Company's products, but there were not a large number of them, and no pendulum models were included. The only American firm included in this catalogue was Ansonia, and all the models shown were pendulum clocks, so there was no competition in connection with balance clocks here, but a range was offered from one of the German factories whose products form the bulk of the catalogue, and it was typical of the selection that would have been offered by an American firm at the time. The German clocks were cheaper than the British United models, but the German firm did not offer a miniature clock such as the Bee or the Gnat, nor did they offer a carriage clock, as British United did. The carriage clock was offered with a white or ivory dial and in a nickel or gilt case, but it was in a much lower price-bracket than the French carriage clocks.

A mystery which has not yet been solved is the origin of movements marked 'Caledonian'. They are seen in drop-dials and also on clocks of the mirror type mentioned in connection with Holloway & Co. Sometimes a highly coloured paper is in the back of the case. The movement is in the lyre shape associated with Seth Thomas, but it has been proved that the parts of a Caledonian movement are not interchangeable with a Seth Thomas movement. It has been suggested that this movement was a product of British United, and investigations are still continuing. This is an example of the type of research that collecting American clocks can lead to.

Clocks have been seen with movements marked 'Jerome & Co' and 'New Haven Clock Co' and the words 'British Made'. Rumour has it that an assembly-plant was located in Liverpool. (A directory entry of 1884 gives 159 Victoria Street.) The clocks were of similar design and appeared to date from the present century. The cases opened at the back, and rear pendulums were provided. 'Jerome & Co' existed as a British Company for selling clocks and remained in business after Chauncey Jerome's own failure. Thereafter the firm dealt mainly with New Haven Clock Company, which acquired the Jerome firm in 1904.

AMERICAN IMITATIONS

As well as American clocks being imitated outside America, a certain amount of imitation was carried on in the United States itself. The long-case clock was virtually dead by 1830, having been driven off the market by the products of the Connecticut clock-factories. In 1876 Henry C. Work composed the song known as 'My Grandfather's Clock', which has given the long-case clock its popular name. At the time the song was composed, the term 'My Grandfather's Clock' would have referred to something from the distant past in America. In Britain, however, especially in Wales and to a lesser extent in Scotland, the type was still being made, and the popular song would have suggested size rather than age in connection with the word 'Grandfather'.

The E. Howard Company of Boston issued a catalogue in 1888 of 'Hall Striking Clocks', mentioned in the preface that the type had been developed for several years, and even used the term 'Grandfather's Clock', which suggests that the song had aroused the firm's interest in the type. The movements could be made as a timepiece, time and strike with hours only, striking hours and half-hours, hours and quarters, hours and ding-dong quarters and Westminster or Cambridge chimes or both. There is some mystery here, for Westminster and Cambridge chimes are the same. Later in the catalogue it mentions Westminster chimes on wire gongs and Cambridge chimes on saucer gongs, but judging by what other makers have offered, it may be that the so-called Cambridge chimes were on eight bells in contrast to the Westminster on four gongs.

Only one of these clocks bears a resemblance to a British or American long-case clock of the traditional type, and that is the cheapest. The others are in late-Victorian Gothic styles and have the weights and pendulum visible through glass so common on modern reproductions. The clocks are all very large with dials at least 13 inches in diameter, and some are provided with moon-phase. Where the weights are visible, they are in brass cases. Graham dead-beat escapements and maintaining-power are a standard feature of all models.

The Waltham Clock Company in 1910 issued a catalogue which included a number of long-case reproductions. All have visible pendulum and weights, and the cases tended to be deeper, especially on the models which had tubular bells for the chime. The designs differ very little from the long-case reproductions of today.

The Waltham Clock Company are also offering clocks with marble dials, such as were included in the Howard catalogue of 1874. The descriptive matter suggests that the clocks have become very popular, but none of the other firms seems to have taken an interest in them. The new models include dead-beat escapements, maintaining-power and stopwork, as do the reproduction Banjo clocks offered by the firm. The latter appear to be very close copies of the original design and well finished.

The Waterbury catalogue for 1908 illustrates no fewer than six designs of Banjo clock, each of which can be offered as a weight-driven timepiece or a spring-driven striking-clock. This catalogue includes a number of long-case clocks, none of which really approaches the traditional designs.

The Howard Banjo clocks which appeared in the catalogue for 1874 must be among the earliest reproductions of American designs, but while the basic idea of the movement is copied, the finish is different from the Willard design. Other firms, such as the Sessions Clock Company which succeeded E. N. Welch, produced spring-driven Banjo clocks, but they are not particularly faithful to the prototype.

One of the biggest surprises in the way of a reproduction clock is in the St Louis Clock and Silverware catalogue for 1904. This is a model called 'Putnam', but it is a new version of the 'Bronze Looking-Glass Clock' of the late 1820s and is even weight-driven, although it runs for eight days and strikes on a cathedral bell. The carving of the ornaments is by hand. The clock is spoilt by its dial which is in the Art Nouveau style.

During the late nineteenth century a lot of imitation of contemporary designs was going on in the American factories. Similar designs turn up in the catalogues of more than one factory and are usually given different names. Not only did the American factories imitate each other's products but they looked to the Continent for inspiration as well, and the number of bronze-cased clocks with statuettes for their decoration suggests French work of the early-nineteenth century, and the contemporary imitations of the French marble clocks are well known. The American factories also produced their own version of the Vienna Regulator and then went further and produced their own developments of the design. Precision Regulators, such as are used by watchmakers and observatories, were also produced in America, some of them having movements imported from Switzerland, but the style of the clock is European.

8　Repairs

As it becomes progressively more difficult to get a clock repaired, the collector is given greater incentive to perform his own repairs on the clocks he acquires. There is not a great deal of difficulty in the work, but it cannot be learned in five minutes, and it is better to practise on some broken movements which are of little value before a piece from one's own collection is attempted. There are a number of textbooks on the subject of clock-repairing, and it is a good plan to read as many of these as possible to get an idea of the principles involved before the work is tackled in earnest.

For many years now American movements have not been welcome with professional clock-repairers. Most of them are in very run-down condition on account of their comparatively long working-life, and they were never intended to be anything but cheap when they were made. The work can be very time-consuming and a real labour of love that would be fantastically expensive if man-hours had to be costed. Luckily a certain amount of material is available, although nothing like as much as there was years ago, and with the aid of a reasonable kit of tools, and possibly a small lathe, wonders can be performed.

The kit of tools does not have to be elaborate. Most of the textbooks suggest various items that should form the basic equipment, and this should include pliers, files, a small hacksaw, some abrasive paper, tweezers, a filing-block and a pinvice with one or two spare chucks. As time goes on, the items can be added to, and various useful additions can be self-made. It is a good plan to hoard all small pieces of wire that are found, as it is a most useful commodity for making taper-pins, hooks for weights, a hook for guiding weight-lines into position and many other things. Pegwood is needed for cleaning, and that sold by material-dealers is made from dogwood, but a good substitute is twigs from a willow tree, the kind that is used for making cricket-bats, and this will do the job quite well, although it is softer than the dogwood.

If a wooden movement has to be dealt with, it is necessary to have fretsaws which can be used in the frame of a piercing-saw as it is shorter and less fatiguing to operate than a normal fretsaw frame. Various grades of glasspaper are needed and a set of carving chisels.

Scotch glue is usually recommended for veneer, but modern glues contained in a plastic bottle and applied with a nozzle are easier to work with on the components of a movement.

REPAIRING WOODEN MOVEMENTS

It is unlikely that many British readers will have to deal with wooden movements, but these are not so rare in America, and therefore a few notes on the subject of repair are included. Extreme care is necessary, and it is an advantage to have had some experience handling metal movements before a wooden one is attempted. The parts of a wood movement are much larger but they can be very brittle and have to be handled gently. The plates of the clock are made of pieces of oak about 6–12 millimetres ($\frac{1}{4}$–$\frac{1}{2}$ inch) thick, well seasoned and with a straight grain. If the movement is to be durable, only the best quality wood should be used, and it is a good plan to build up a stock of all kinds of pieces of wood of a good quality that might be useful. This can be obtained from old timber from houses that are being demolished, old pieces of furniture and so on. The major requirement is that the wood should be properly seasoned, have a good grain and be dry, but not so dry that it cracks every time it is handled.

On the old clocks, the wheels were of cherry and the pinions of laurel. A good substitute is boxwood for pinions on account of its hardness, and a possible source of supply is old chessmen. While one would hesitate to break up a complete set, there is no harm in using material from a set that is already incomplete. The pillars of the movement will probably not need renewal, but if new pillars are to be made, then a lathe is indispensable. New arbors also require a lathe for their making.

If it is required to make a new arbor with its pinion, a piece of wood should be selected that is slightly longer than the space between the plates and large enough to accommodate the outside diameter of the pinion leaves. It can then be trimmed to a length of about $1\frac{1}{2}$ millimetres ($\frac{1}{16}$ inch) less than the distance between the plates. The wood should be shaped with chisels until it is roughly circular, remembering to leave enough material where the pinion leaves come and at the place for the wheel-seating. Turning is best done on a metal turning-lathe which is provided with large collets or a self-centring chuck. One end of the wood is trimmed to fit the collet or chuck firmly, and then the other end is finished in the lathe using a metal turning-graver in preference to wood turning-tools. Do not turn completely to finished size. The work should not rotate too fast, and light cuts should be taken. Having turned one end of the arbor, the work should be drilled from the tailstock to receive the wire for the pivot and can then be reversed and the other end turned. The portion where the leaves are to come is also turned, leaving it somewhat large. The second hole for the wire pivot can be drilled and the pivots inserted at each end, allowing the pivots themselves to be fractionally longer than the thickness of the plate and the depth of the hole being at least $1\frac{1}{2}$ times this length. The work is now remounted using the pivots as centres, and it will now require to be supported at the tailstock end as well. The finishing cuts can now be made, bringing the arbor to its correct size and taking particular care of the wheel-seating. When the finishing cut is made on the portion where the leaves come, there should still be some extra material left which can be eliminated as the leaves are cut.

If the lathe has an indexing-head, the cylindrical portion where the leaves come can be marked with as many horizontal lines as there are to be leaves. The tool-rest is brought as near to the centre line of the wood as possible and a pencil-mark made using the top of the tool-rest as a straight edge while the index-plate is moved the correct number of divisions for the number of leaves required. The arbor is then removed from the lathe and the leaf-portion held end to end in a vice with wooden clams protecting the jaws and the marks used to guide a fine saw until the cut has been made to the correct depth of the leaf. When all the saw cuts have been made, they are opened out with woodcarving chisels until the leaves are approximately the right size, and then they are finished with a fine file and glasspaper. The operative ends of the leaves must be carefully rounded and smooth, and it is a matter of trial and error to make sure that the pinion meshes properly with its adjacent wheel when the arbors are mounted in the plates. The secret of the job is patience. Once the pinion runs correctly, the wheel can be mounted on the portion of the arbor reserved for it, and then a test is made to see that it also runs true and meshes correctly with its adjacent pinion.

It is not very likely that a wheel will need entire replacement but more than likely that some teeth may have broken off. The broken teeth are cut away from the rim of the wheel and a dovetailed portion cut below to receive a piece of wood slightly thicker than the wheel. This piece of wood is glued into position, and when it is dry, the teeth can be marked in pencil and cut with a fretsaw, finishing them with a file and glasspaper. The nature of a wooden wheel means that some of the teeth have to be cut with the grain and some across the grain. John Harrison, the pioneer of the marine chronometer, made a number of clocks with wooden wheels and was always careful to build them up in segments so that the pressure while the clock was working would not act along the grain and tend to push part of the tooth off. The American clocks always had their wheels made out of one piece of wood as the purpose of their manufacture was cheapness, and it will usually be found that where the teeth have sheared, they are cut across the grain. The new piece of wood should therefore be inserted so that the grain runs parallel to the teeth if maximum strength is desired, but if it is more important to the owner of the clock to restore the wheel as near its former appearance as possible, then the grain should go the other way. When the wheel has been tested in the clock and found to mesh correctly with its adjacent pinion, then the extra thickness can be removed from the inset portion and the wood treated to bring it as near as possible to the original colour, by using either stain or a small quantity of linseed oil.

Pieces of a wooden hang-up movement. Note several broken teeth.

It should be noted that the teeth of American wooden wheels lean forward slightly. This is done to reduce friction with the solid pinions used. Teeth on wooden wheels of clocks from the Black Forest which employ lantern-pinions are usually made upright. When cutting teeth it is important that the saw be held correctly so that the tooth is the same size on both sides of the wheel. A power-operated saw would take care of this matter, which becomes increasingly difficult the thicker the blank from which the wheel is cut.

Only those parts which are made of metal and rub-on metal should be oiled on a wooden clock movement, i.e. pallets, scapewheel arbor, pallet-bearing and crutch where it embraces the pendulum-rod. These parts are mentioned in the standard wording of the paper that was used in OGs. Where the pivots run in holes in the wooden plates, they are left dry. Lifting-pieces usually have wooden pivots working in wooden holes, and these also run dry. It is important that all holes are clean, and they should be pegged out as on a metal movement.

If holes have worn very large, a plug of hard wood should be inserted after the hole has been broached out and drilled to admit the pivot. It should be remembered that the amount of play in a wooden movement is much greater than on a metal one, and the large size of the teeth means that there is more tolerance on depthing.

The assembly of a wooden movement is not as easy as it may appear, in spite of the large size of the parts. On a hang-up movement the pallets may be inserted into the main frame at the same time as the wheels, and this means another arbor to replace every time the plates are eased open to adjust the position of the wheels of the striking-train. As on other clocks, it is important that the locking takes place immediately after the hammer has fallen. The instant of locking is usually controlled by a cam on the Continental principle rather than the hoop-wheel found on British clocks, and the cam may have two slots, an anticipation of the brass clocks of the second half of the nineteenth century that were made by such firms as Ansonia.

The book on Eli Terry by Kenneth D. Roberts mentioned in the Bibliography contains a number of views of movements of wooden clocks and will give a good idea of what the various parts look like if it is necessary to replace a part that is missing. On a shelf-clock movement the scapewheel projects through the front plate, but the pallets are usually separate and do not have to be put in place until the rest of the movement has been put together. There are exceptions to this, such as the Silas Hoadley 'Upside Down' movement and the Boardman 'Groaner'.

The flat springs holding barrels and main wheels together can be expected to be formed of tinplate, and if they need replacement, it is not a difficult task to make them. The 'pins' holding the plates together can be filed up from pegwood using a filing-block, and the taper should be nice and gentle. Replacement of pallets will be dealt with when repairs to brass movements are being discussed.

REPAIRING METAL MOVEMENTS: THE OG

One of the best movements for the beginner in clock-repairing to deal with is the OG. The parts are fairly robust, there are not too many of them, and the movement is large enough to see what is going on fairly clearly. In addition there are no mainsprings to worry about.

Let us assume that a very battered OG has been acquired and that repairs to the movement are about to be made. The first step is to remove the taper-pin that holds the hands on and take off the minute-hand, which should be quite loose. The hour-hand is held by a short tube and needs a little pressure to bring it up, but it should not give any trouble. The dial can then be unscrewed or unpinned as the case may be, and the movement is then visible. It will be held on to a small seatboard by means of iron hooks which are secured by nuts below. The seatboard fits into grooves in the two side-partitions, and the cords for the weights pass through spaces in the partitions and over pulleys in the top of the case. It is more than likely that the weights have been tied on to the cords, which is incorrect, and as the cords ought to be replaced as a matter of routine, there is no harm in cutting the cords just above the knots and taking the weights off. If the clock is wound up, the weights will be next to the movement, and it will be necessary to let them down before they can be removed. On the going side all that is necessary is to turn aside the wire that holds the pallets on their stud, remove the pallets and let the train run until the weight is low enough. Repeated raising of the lifting-piece on the striking-side will lower the striking weight.

This method assumes that both trains are free to run, which is not always the case, and a careful inspection should be made to see if the reason is simply dirt, in which case some penetrating-oil applied to each pivot will soften the dirt after an hour or two. If the trains are held because of a mechanical interruption, a careful inspection should be made until the trouble is located. It might be from a variety of reasons, including bent pivots, bent wheels fouling the frame or the barrels, broken or shifted lantern-pinions, or bent lifting-pieces interrupting the wheels or the fly. Force should not be used to free the trains. When the weights have been removed, the cords should be pulled back through the holes in the top of the case and through the partitions. It is useful to make a hook on a piece of wire about 15 centimetres (6 inches) long for doing this. The block of wood with a groove in its side that supports the top edge of the movement back-plate should be unscrewed, and the pins which pass through the sides of the holes in the seatboard and enter the partitions should come out. If they are not broken, they can be eased out with long-nose pliers. The movement can now be slid forward and the case put aside in a safe place until it is required.

When taking a movement down, it is useful to have a number of receptacles for the various parts, especially if the movement is a complicated one. Two-ounce tobacco-tins and the cardboard or plastic trays in which items are purchased from supermarkets are useful for this purpose. The first step in dismantling is to unscrew the nuts which fasten the seatboard-hooks and detach the movement from the seatboard. The nuts can then be screwed back on to their hooks and put into a stoppered glass jar which will eventually receive all the small parts for soaking.

The plates are held together by tapered pins pushed through holes in the pillars or more rarely by nuts. It sometimes happens that the pins are almost rusted through, and on pressure being applied with pliers they bend and break. If this occurs, the protruding ends can be filed off using a file with a safe edge which is placed next to the plate. When the clock is all in pieces, the stumps remaining can be pushed out with a fine punch or, if the corrosion is very bad, the holes can be re-drilled. During this operation the stumps may come free and render it unnecessary to carry on with the drilling right to the end.

The most important thing to observe before the parts are removed is the position of the lifting-pieces. One is embraced between the wires of the other, and it is important that they are replaced correctly. A most important tool in any workshop is a scrap-pad with a pencil to make notes of details such as this. The plates can now be separated and the wheels removed. The barrels should be removed from the main wheels by pressing out the tiny pins that hold them next to the tension-springs. These pins are made short to fit in the groove that is stamped into the tension-springs, which are made of brass and are usually in the form of a trefoil. A similar fastening is used for the thick wheel on the centre arbor that is driven by the main wheel. Once again, the small parts go in the glass jar.

The clicks should be inspected at this stage and are almost certain to want tightening. A few taps with a light hammer on the rear side of the rivet will probably be all that is required, and it is easy to overdo this tightening and make the click so stiff that the return spring is unable to move it. A click too tight can be loosened by gripping it with pliers and working it to and fro with plenty of oil. The clicksprings should be inspected and re-bent if necessary to increase their tension. They are among the most important parts of the clock and MUST be made to give reliable service. If any doubt is felt, replace the clickspring with a new one bent up out of a suitable piece of wire. The end of the click itself must comfortably fit the ratchet teeth, and a few touches with a fine file will help here. When replacing the tension-springs, they should have their vanes bent a little to increase the tension. This is a convenient time to test the pins for raising the hammer. Sometimes one or more work loose, and they can be tightened by holding the operating end of the pin on a vice or anvil and giving a few taps with a punch on the rear end to spread the metal a fraction.

The lantern-pinions should be inspected for excessive wear, and if necessary they can be shifted a little along their arbor so that a different portion of the wires is operated upon by the adjacent wheel. A hollow punch is necessary for this operation and is quite easy to make from brass or steel rod. The hole should be of a size to accommodate the pivot comfortably without being too tight, and the opposite end of the arbor goes between the jaws of the vice which are opened just enough to receive it, with the lantern-pinion resting on top. A scratch should be made on the arbor where it is desired that the lantern-pinion should stop, and light taps should be given to the punch until the correct position is reached. The relevant parts should then be inserted in the plates for testing and any adjustment made. If it is desired to move the lantern-pinion away from a wheel located at the other end of the arbor, the pinion has to be supported by a stake which can overhang the jaws of the vice sufficiently to clear the wheel. This can be made by cutting a notch in the end of a strip of iron, fastening the latter tightly in the vice so that there is enough overhang and then resting the lantern-pinion on the metal surrounding the notch with the arbor going through the centre. The hollow punch is then applied and the work tried in the frame of the clock as before.

The fly is held to its arbor by a small wire which allows it to overrun as locking takes place and absorb shock, and also keeps the fly at the right position on its arbor so it does not foul other parts of the movement as it rotates. This little wire sometimes gets weak and needs tightening. The cam on the second arbor should be inspected for looseness and tightened if necessary, although this is rarely required. Work on the going side is usually only the shifting of lantern-pinions.

The pivots will almost certainly be worn and the holes in which they run need rebushing. The first step is to trim the pivots, and this can be done on a filing-block holding the other end of the arbor in a pinvice, or more easily in a lathe. A series of pivot-beds should be made if a Jacot drum is not available. A piece of silver steel about 6 millimetres ($\frac{1}{4}$ inch) in diameter is drilled in the lathe with a hole approximately the diameter of a pivot to a depth of 10 millimetres ($\frac{3}{8}$ inch). Half the diameter of the steel is filed away for a distance longer than the depth of the hole, leaving the remains of the hole as a concave bed in a flat surface. Several of these beds should be made using different diameters of drill, and the length of each piece should be about 3 centimetres ($1\frac{1}{4}$ inches). When all the pieces are ready, they should be hardened and tempered (straw). When the pieces are held in the tailstock of the lathe with the pivot supported by the bed, pressure can be applied to the pivot while it rotates without fear of its breaking off. The pivot is smoothed with a pivot-file and afterwards burnished with a burnisher, and when all pivots have been dealt with, the holes in which they run can be re-bushed.

'American' bushes are sold by material-dealers in boxes and range from 3 millimetres ($\frac{1}{8}$ inch) long with an outside diameter of 1–2 millimetres ($\frac{1}{24}$–$\frac{1}{12}$ inch). When dealing with an OG movement, it is sometimes necessary to use 'English' bushes, as they are larger and provide for pivots of greater size than the 'American' bushes, which are more suitable for the eight-day movements of the Ansonia type. The plates of American clocks are thinner than those of the normal British long-case movement, and if the bushes are hammered in violently and the hole is near the edge of the plate, the hole may burst. It is therefore necessary to broach the old hole as carefully as

A tablet from an OG by E. N. Welch, *c.* 1870 and modern
version

A modern pictorial tablet

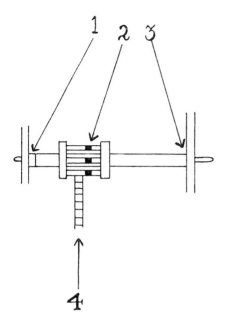

Shifting a pinion to avoid the
worn part of the leaves.
  1. Collet inserted.
  2. Worn part of leaves.
  3. Shoulder which is turned
  back.
  4. Wheel.

possible until the bush almost fits right through and then secure it
with light, even blows of the hammer. If the worst happens and the
hold does burst, then a little soft solder should be applied. The bushes
for main arbors are much larger and longer than those for the rest of
the train, and it is these that are being referred to when the clock-
paper says 'Extra Bushed'. An American frame is not so rigid as a
British one, and the pivots should therefore have more play to allow
for a slight movement in the frame.

Many American clocks are provided with very long pivots, and it is
sometimes possible to allow for very worn wires in the lantern-
pinions by cutting back the shoulder on one end of the arbor and
making a tiny steel collet for the other end. Clearance of the various
parts will usually determine which arbor is operated on. If the
amount of metal available does not allow this to happen by adjusting
one arbor only, then it is sometimes possible to spread the
adjustment over two arbors using opposite ends. It is better to adjust
arbors by this method than to insert a bush and leave it proud, for the
latter method brings in complications when assembling. If the pivots
do not allow adjustment to be made in this way, then the shifting of
the lantern-pinion has to take place as described previously. Another
method of adjustment if the wires are not loose is to turn each one
through half a turn using fine, long nose-pliers.

A lantern-pinion can have its wires renewed by turning off the side
where the shroud has been riveted over to secure the wires in place.
New wires need not be of a steel up to the quality of pivot steel. It is

much easier to work with wire that is easier to cut and bears more relation to the wire used originally. This wire will last for years and can be easily renewed when it has worn. The tapered pins sold by material-dealers are useful for this purpose. When the new wires are in place, the end of the shroud should be smoothed and a brass collet put on with soft solder. The original fastening would have been by punching over the ends of the holes through which the wires were inserted, but this is best done by machinery, and also the shroud has been weakened a little by turning some of it off to release the old wires.

If it is desired to tighten or replace the pin on which the pallets ride, it should be done before the clock is cleaned. The best material is pivot steel, and it should be fixed by punching the brass round it after it has been put into place.

When repairs have been completed, the movement can be cleaned. It is not often that an OG has to be bushed all the way through, but the second arbor on the going-train will often be found to have worn its holes, and the scapewheel especially must run true in order to avoid errors in the action of the escapement.

Cleaning is best done by immersing the parts of the movement in a solution of soap to which some household ammonia has been added. The soap-solution is prepared by saving scraps of soap from household use and boiling a handful of them in about a litre of water. When it is cool, a jelly will form which should be stored in a stoppered vessel. When cleaning a clock, three or four tablespoons of this jelly to a litre of water should be sufficient. The household ammonia is added as soon as the parts have been put into the soap-solution, three or four tablespoons being enough. Soaking-time varies according to the state of the clock, but frequent inspections will reveal how cleaning is going on. The solution should be kept covered while soaking is in progress. Small parts should have been stored in a stoppered glass jar, and this can be filled with enough solution to cover the parts. At no time should any part have any of its surface exposed to the air, or a tidemark will form that is difficult to eradicate.

When the parts have soaked long enough, they should be removed from the solution (count them as they go in and see that none are left behind when they are removed) and rinsed. Very fine steel wool can be used to remove the dirt, or the plastic scourers used in the kitchen for cleaning saucepans do quite well. Heavy scrubbing is not required if soaking has been sufficient. Drying with a clean rag and

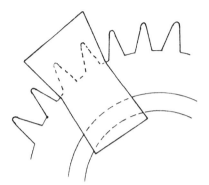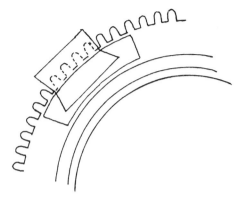

Inserting new teeth in wooden and brass wheels. The latter shows the reinforcing-strip to be soldered on.

brushing with a dry brush should give sufficient finish. If the clock has a large hole in the centre of the dial, the front plate and any parts that show through the hole should be polished with metal-polish.

After the plates and wheels are clean, the holes should be pegged out and the barrels and main wheels and the centre arbor and its driving-wheel put together with their tension-springs. At this stage the count-wheel is put on its stud and secured by its tension-spring being slid into position. It may happen that the teeth of the main wheel are cut to about half their thickness through wear, although this is more common in spring-clocks. This can be corrected by reversing the wheel and re-fastening the clickwork on the opposite side. On an OG the barrel and wheel are fastened by a taper-pin and the tension-spring, but on spring-driven clocks the fastening may be by means of a brass or steel collet which has been riveted on and can be removed only by breaking the riveting carefully, leaving enough metal remaining for the riveting to take place a second time. At this stage it is convenient to check the wire securing the pallets on the wire on which they ride and see that it remains firm when sprung into position.

If one or more teeth are broken off a wheel, the rim of the wheel is cut out in a dovetail as was done in the repair of a wooden wheel, but the thinness of the brass makes it difficult to hammer in the new piece on which the teeth are to be cut. The new piece should be cut and filed to fit the hole as closely as possible, and a thin strip of brass as wide as the rim of the wheel less the teeth and longer than the new piece should be laid over it, and the whole fastened by soft solder. The teeth can then be cut by a fine file, and on account of the thinness of the metal, it is helpful to back up the metal being cut with a very thin piece of wood placed with the wheel between the jaws of the vice.

RE-ASSEMBLY: THE OG

Assembly begins by placing the back plate of the movement on a wooden box without a lid so that the plate is supported at its edges and the pivots have room to protrude. All arbors except the scape-arbor are put into their holes in the back plate, not forgetting the lifting-pieces and the hammer. It is important to note where the various arms of the lifting-pieces come in relation to the wheels and also to each other. The top plate can now be put in place with the scapewheel having its front pivot inserted in its hole. The scape-arbor must be guided down into its proper place, and the barrel and centre arbors will meet the plate first and help to steady the plate as the other arbors get near to their position. A certain amount of confusion may take place as the pivots are placed in their holes, and the lifting-pieces may fall out and get caught in other parts of the clock, but it is just a matter of patience, and each clock done is easier than the last.

Having got all the pivots in position, the plates should be pinned together and the striking tried. There will be a spring for the hammer that is either fixed to the back plate and hooks on to a special wire on the hammer-arbor or else is in the form of a coil and hooks on to the edge of the plate. If the clock is a Brewster single-pin strike, there will be no problem with setting the striking except to ensure that the fly is able to move about half a turn when the clock warns. If the hammer is actuated by pins on the great wheel, the position of the second arbor in relation to the great wheel must be so arranged that the lifting-piece arm falls into the slot in the cam immediately after the hammer has fallen. This is adjusted by unpinning the plate and turning the second arbor in relation to the great wheel until this process occurs correctly. In the locked position the fly should be ready to run about half a turn at warning, and it is not much trouble to unpin the plates and adjust the fly in relation to the second arbor.

The pallets do not have to be put on until the movement is

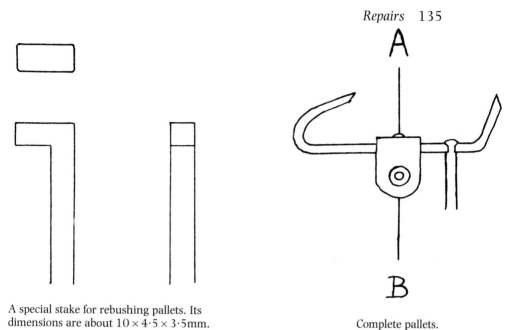

A special stake for rebushing pallets. Its
dimensions are about $10 \times 4 \cdot 5 \times 3 \cdot 5$mm.

Complete pallets.

Pallets (left) with an extra piece of brass
fastened inside. The dotted lines indicate
the centre for drilling holes. Pallets (right)
being rebushed using a bush with cap and
special stake. The dotted lines show the
section A/B on the illustration above right.

The crutch wire before
riveting into the steel strip.

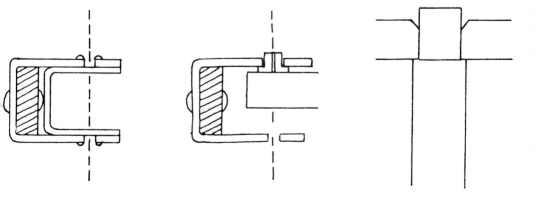

assembled. They ride on a piece of wire mounted on an adjustable arm so that the depth can be corrected and are kept from working off by a springy piece of wire that fits over the end of the wire carrying them. The end of the retaining-wire is flattened and made slightly bowed so that it does not readily move after it has been sprung in place. Care should be taken that it does not rub against the brass piece supporting the pallets.

The pallets will probably have worn the holes in the brass piece which supports them. This can be corrected by inserting a tiny bush either side with the aid of a small L-shaped piece of steel that is held in the vice and acts as a miniature anvil. An easier method is to fold a three-sided shape out of a brass strip to fit inside the existing support and be soldered and then insert a piece of wood of the same thickness as the space in the middle in order to support the work when drilling. The old holes show the position for drilling the new ones.

If the holes are not too worn, the problem may be overcome by removing the pin on which the pallets ride and inserting a thicker one. This should be done before the movement is assembled. This pin should be tightly fixed in the small arm that moves to allow adjustment for depthing, and the holes in the brass are then broached to fit it. If this pin is made longer than previously and a small collet put on first, the pallets will be acted upon by the wheel at a different place, and this will form a good way of compensating for wear if it is not desired to make new pallets. The latter job is not, however, as difficult as it may seem. A piece of steel stock is taken longer and thicker than the finished pallets are to be. The steel is bent to the shape shown in the drawing so that the finished pallets embrace eight teeth of the wheel plus half a space when the steel has been reduced to its proper length.

A hole is then drilled in the centre for receiving the rivet that holds the brass piece on which the pallets ride and another half way between the centre and the bend on the 'Exit' side which will receive the crutch-wire. This hole should be chamfered on the side which comes inside the pallets. The sides of the steel are now filed to the correct width, remembering that the thickness of the brass carrier on each side and the width of the steel added together must be fractionally less than the length of the wire on which the pallets ride.

The brass piece is made from a strip about 5 millimetres ($\frac{1}{5}$ inch) wide and something less than a millimetre thick. It is bent in two places using the steel piece as a former, and the two sides are trimmed to a length of 6 millimetres ($\frac{1}{4}$ inch) from the bends. The corners should be rounded and the centre hole for the rivet drilled, after which the working-holes are drilled in the sidepieces, while a piece of thin wood cut to the thickness of the space between the two sides is used as a support. The holes are broached to fit the wire, and then the brass piece is riveted to the steel with the rivet-head below and the new head formed on top.

The crutch-wire is made from brass; suitable pieces of brass wire are sold by material-dealers, about 15 centimetres (6 inches) long and 1.5 millimetres ($\frac{1}{16}$ inch) thick. The lower end is filed to a gentle taper for about 3 centimetres ($1\frac{1}{4}$ inches) using a pinvice and filing-block. The purpose of this is to make the wire of less diameter where it embraces the pendulum-rod to reduce friction. The other end of the wire is filed to a smaller diameter for about 3 millimetres ($\frac{1}{8}$ inch), and when it is inserted in the steel portion, there should be enough metal protruding to allow a rivet to be made that fills the countersink. When the wire is fixed, the ends of the pallets should be filed to approximately correct length and the pallets and wheel tried together. A certain amount of filing and bending will be necessary, and the angles of the pallets should be such that each tooth strikes either pallet at approximately the same distance from its end, and the drop or distance moved by the wheel each time is equal. The under-surface of each pallet is chamfered so that the tooth escapes cleanly. When the pallets will keep moving while pressure is applied to the train, they can be considered correct. A final check can be made by causing them to move fast and looking at the positions taken up by the scapewheel teeth. A stroboscopic effect takes place, and if the pallets are correct, the images of the teeth should appear equidistant from each other. If the brass piece and the crutch-wire are firm, the steel can then be hardened and the acting-surfaces of the pallets finished with fine emery with the final strokes in the direction that the teeth will rub on the pallet. After the pallets have been cleaned, the crutch is formed at the tapered end of the wire. The wire is turned at a right angle and passes behind the pendulum-rod, bends forward and returns. The loop should be small enough not to lose power as the clock runs, but it should not be so tight that there is unnecessary friction. On an American movement the point where the pendulum is suspended and the centre of the pallets are somewhat distant from each other, so there is a certain amount of friction as the crutch-loop slides up and down the pendulum-rod.

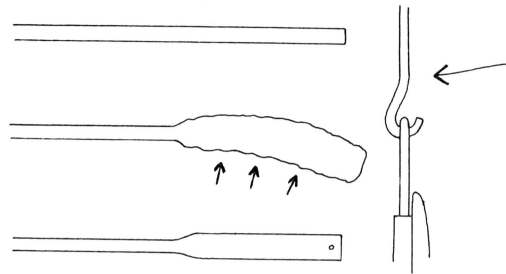

Left: The three stages in making a pendulum-rod. The arrows indicate the places to hammer to correct curvature. Right: The bob hooked on to the end of the pendulum wire. The arrow indicates the bend to enable the bob to hang on the centre line.

Special cord used to be sold for American clocks, and it is hoped that a supply will soon be available again. In the meantime, a nylon cord is suitable, provided it is thin enough. When the clock is fully wound, the cord should form only one layer on the barrel. It is fastened by a simple knot in the larger end of the hole through the barrel. Small hooks should be made to take the weights so that they can be readily lifted on or off. The hooks should not be too long, or difficulty will be found in getting them threaded on to the loops in the tops of the weights.

The pendulum-rod is made of wire about $1\frac{1}{2}$ millimetres ($\frac{1}{16}$ inch) in diameter, and the suspension-spring is beaten out at one end. Material-dealers now stock them, but they are easy to make oneself. The end of the wire is made red hot for about 4 centimetres ($1\frac{1}{2}$ inches) and rapidly beaten flat as it cools very quickly. As beating proceeds, the flattened portion may curve off the centre line, but this can be corrected by hammering on the inside of the curve. When the metal has been formed into a thin strip, it should be fixed in the vice and filed on both edges, using the vice-jaw as a guide for straightness. The surfaces are then filed with a fine file, using a filing-block with the round portion of the wire resting in a groove, and finished with abrasive paper. At this stage it is very easy to damage the spring, so care is needed when filing and smoothing. The spring should not be too stiff or the clock will stop. A very tiny hole is then made with a sharp punch at the end of the spring to secure it in the block that supports it. A thin wire is threaded through the hole and cut off about 3 millimetres ($\frac{1}{8}$ inch) each side, after which it is bent parallel to the surface of the spring. When the spring has been inserted in the stud and pulled down until the wire rests on the top, the sides of the stud are closed with steady pressure from large pliers. German clocks often have the hole in the spring made larger and drilled so that the spring is secured by a taper-pin that passes right through the stud.

The pendulum must not swing obliquely to the front plate as this increases friction and may stop the clock. The trouble can be caused by the suspension-spring being twisted or the stud being bent. The pendulum-wire must not touch the front or back of the crutch-loop, and the portion of the rod where the crutch-loop rubs should be smoothed with emery in the longitudinal direction. The hook at the bottom of the pendulum must face the front squarely, and if it does

Spare pendulum-bobs and pallets. Note the shape of the wire for fitting in the bob.

not do so, it can be corrected by twisting the hook with a pair of pliers while the wire is held very firmly by another pair as high up as possible. The hook should be bent back slightly so that the pendulum-bob hangs directly below the pendulum-wire.

Sometimes the length of the pendulum is stamped on the movement, but when a clock's pendulum is missing and a new one has to be provided, the length is calculated by beginning with the wheel that is on the centre arbor, and therefore turns once per hour, and multiplying the teeth by the numbers of the teeth of the rest of the wheels in the train including the scapewheel. The total is multiplied by two, as the scapewheel moves only half a tooth-space every time it is released. This figure is then divided by the product of the number of leaves in the pinions, and the answer gives the number of beats per hour. A table in a horological textbook will then give the length of pendulum required to beat at this speed. There is an important point to be noted in connection with American movements. In many instances the centre arbor does not form part of the train but is driven by a wheel meshing with one of the train-wheels. The calculation leaves the train-wheel out entirely and proceeds on the assumption that the wheel on the centre arbor meshes directly with the next pinion.

As a worked example, the wheels and pinions of a Brewster & Ingrahams Sharp Gothic striking-clock were as follows:

Wheel on centre arbor meshing with main wheel 36
Main wheel 80 (omitted from calculation)
Second wheel 80   pinion 6
Scapewheel 52   pinion 6

$$\frac{36 \times 80 \times 52 \times 2}{6 \times 6} = 8{,}320$$

From the table in Saunier's *Modern Horology*, 8,300 beats per hour require a pendulum 187 millimetres long, so the distance from the bottom of the stud to the centre of the bob should be about this.

If the escapement has been correctly adjusted and all other factors are correct, there should be a good swing to the pendulum. A tick that is too loud means wastage of power. It improves the appearance of the clock if the pendulum-bob has a high polish, especially if it is visible through the glass. Lord Grimthorpe noted that American clocks are more accurate if heavier bobs are provided, but the collector of today will probably not want to replace the original.

The movement of an OG is replaced in its case in the reverse order to removing it. The wire with a hook is used to thread the cords over the pulleys, and the pins holding the seatboard to the partitions are inserted with long nose-pliers. The instructions usually specify the light weight on the strike side of the clock, but there is often little difference between the two. If the clock strikes too fast and the fly is not slipping, a lighter weight could be tried. There is usually a thin wire which hooks into the count-wheel lifting-piece and passes through a loop at the front of the seatboard, hanging down below the dial. This is for releasing the strike when the striking is not in step with the hands. Quite often this wire is missing, but if so, it is a simple matter to thread a wire up through the loop and fasten it with pliers to the loop in the lifting-piece.

Many gongs develop a poor tone over the years, and this is usually due to the gong-wire coming loose in the brass ring that supports it. The wire should be pulled out of the brass, the hole cleaned and the wire reinserted, after which the brass is tapped with a hammer to ensure that the wire is firmly gripped. The screw that holds the brass ring to the iron base should be screwed well home. The hammer should not touch the gong when at rest.

REPAIRING OTHER CLOCKS

The small-spring timepieces are not much more difficult to deal with than an OG except that the spring has to be controlled before the clock is taken to pieces. In the case of an alarm- or striking-clock, there will be two springs to deal with. The spring is wound and a clamp placed on the outside to restrain it, after which the spring is allowed to impel the train and run down as far as it will go while being held by the clamp and there is no more power. The trains can be run under supervision to eliminate the power, or else the spring can be wound until the click is raised and then held by a screwdriver while the ratchet-teeth are allowed to run back under the click half a turn at a time, while the key is firmly held. It is most important that the clock is not dismantled while there is the slightest power, or damage and injury can result. When an eight-day movement is being dealt with, extra care is necessary, for the springs are very strong and can do a great deal of harm. It is a good plan to screw the movement to the bench with the aid of the lugs that secure it in the case. The spring can then be let down in stages, always having a firm grip on the key, which should be a good fit on the winding-square. To be extra safe, two clamps should be put on eight-day springs.

The clamps can be made from iron rod or wire 2, $2\frac{1}{2}$ or 3 millimetres in diameter ($\frac{1}{12}$–$\frac{1}{8}$ inch) and bent into rings with about one quarter left open of $2\frac{1}{2}$, 4 and $5\frac{1}{2}$ centimetres respectively in diameter (1, $1\frac{5}{8}$, $2\frac{1}{4}$ inches). It should be noted, before the movement is taken to pieces, which pillars take the loops of the springs. Before assembling, check the clickwork very carefully as it is most important that it does not fail. Eight-day clocks usually have pegs in the plate to restrain the springs from unwinding too far, but if a spring unwinds suddenly, these pegs are not much help in avoiding damage. Some movements have the pallets between the plates but carried on two swivelling-arms for adjusting the depth of the escapement. To let the train run, these arms can be pushed to one side to remove the pallets from contact with the wheel, but the movement of the wheels should be restrained while this is done, and make sure the pallets are *completely* out of contact before the wheels are allowed to run.

If the movement looks very complicated, before stripping a note can be made of the position of the various parts and a number can be scratched on the rim of each wheel as a guide. Note particularly whether the wheel or the pinion comes nearest to the front plate. Assembly is facilitated by the striking usually being operated by the pin-and-cam method on the same arbor, but where the count-wheel is driven continuously and not gathered tooth by tooth, a little adjustment may be necessary. The count-wheel detent must come straight into the middle of the slot and not rub on either side. The warning-wheel should run about half a turn at warning. If it is expected that the top plate may have to be removed after putting it in place, it is handy to make some temporary fastening-pins which are

A temporary pin.

filed to a taper with a loop on the opposite end. When the trains run properly and the striking locks correctly, the temporary pins can be replaced with permanent ones.

Lubrication should be by proper clock-oil only, as this does not dry so quickly as other oils, and a few drops of turret clock-oil should be put on the mainspring, as this oil is thicker and can stand up to the pressure involved.

Eight-day clocks often have their lifting-pieces assisted with light coiled springs. It is important that the correct position of these is noted before the clock is taken down. It will often be found that the wire from which these springs are made has become brittle and may need replacement.

When the movement has been assembled and everything appears to be in order, the springs can be wound and the clamps removed. As the clamps become loose, they can be guided with pliers and threaded through spaces in the plates. The clock should stand or hang level and be set in beat by bending the crutch one way or the other until the time-intervals between the ticks are equal.

The basic repairs to balance-movements are carried out in the same way as on pendulum-clocks, but one or two extra matters have to be considered. Hairsprings are cleaned by soaking in petrol, but only a very small quantity at a time should be used in a small glass or china pot with a tightly fitting lid. A specially pure form of petrol is sold by material-dealers for this purpose. (Great care should be taken with fire-precautions when using it.) If a hairspring is bent, it can be straightened by means of two pairs of tweezers, or better with a special pair of tweezers having one leg convex and one concave.

If the clock is of the type that has solid-lever pallets, the ends should be polished. If the teeth of the scapewheel are badly worn, it may be necessary to reduce the depth between wheel and pallets by inserting solid bushes and redrilling. If this is done, the rim of the wheel may need reducing slightly to clear the pallets. The tip of the lever must be very close to, but not touching, the balance-staff. If pin-pallets are very cut, they should be renewed, taking care that the new ones are just the same size as the old. Pivot-steel is ideal for the job, but sewing-needles form another source of material. The new pin-pallets are inserted from the back, using a stake for support. If the scapewheel teeth of a pin-pallet escapement are worn, a new wheel is the only remedy.

The screws with hollow ends that support the balance should be

The plate from a BUCC movement; a spare Great Wheel for an OG, with the vendor's label; an Ansonia key and normal key; a barrel arbor with brass surround; two crank-keys for OGs.

checked for wear, and if tiny pits have been ground in the surface, the hole should be drilled a little deeper. If the steel is very hard, the hole can be extended with pegwood and a touch of grinding-paste. Clean up well afterwards. If the balance-pivots are worn, they can be corrected by means of a stone while the balance-staff is rotated in the lathe.

If a balance-clock is out of beat, it is corrected by repinning the hairspring in a new position so that the balance swings to the same amount each side of the lever.

As a final warning, the importance of not removing the clamps until everything appears to be in order and the plates firmly fastened together should be stressed. It is better to err on the side of caution than to have to contend with accidents or damage.

9 The Restoration of Cases and Dials

The case of an old American clock that has been acquired may be in a very decrepit state and have suffered anything from fire-damage to being stored in a chicken-run. The first thing to do when restoring a case is to take out the movement and keep it in a safe place until it is ready to be repaired. Most American clocks allow the movement to be removed from the front after the dial and hands have been taken off, but the 'Beehive' is an exception, and the back of the case has to be unscrewed, after which the movement can be taken out. The rear pendulum-movements used in imitation-marble cases also come out from the rear, while those clocks with porcelain cases may have to have them removed from below after the bottom has been unscrewed.

THE CASE

The dirt is removed from a case having a veneered finish with a very fine steel wool using either a 50/50 mixture of turpentine and linseed oil (white spirit is a good substitute for turpentine) or a paint-brush cleaner (NOT paint-stripper). The case may have been covered with varnish stain from time to time, and this must all be removed with the steel wool and the mixture. Try the effect of a little methylated spirit on the varnish stain in a remote corner to see if it is worth proceeding with as a solvent. If the case is French-polished, it will remove the polish also, and a decision should be made whether the cleaning should proceed using this solvent or not. If so, the case will need to be French-polished again when it has been cleaned. The basic method of cleaning is for the steel wool to be moistened with the mixture and a small area cleaned, after which it is dried with a clean rag. The finishing strokes should be in the direction of the grain, especially on OG mouldings. Care is needed when dealing with the door as the glass tablet is very vulnerable. When the case is being cleaned, it is often better to remove the door with the tablet and put it in a safe place. Cleaners containing water should not be used.

Cases that are made of wood or iron and finished to imitate marble are best cleaned by using a pad of cotton wool and white spirit only. Steel wool might remove some of the paint which provides the

A Seth Thomas OG as found (left) and restored (right).

marbling effect or scratch the black finish on iron cases. If an iron case is chipped here and there, it may have formed some rust-patches which should be removed, but no abrasive should be used. There are several rust-removers on the market, and one spot should be treated first and observed after a few days to see the effect before doing the entire case.

The interior of the case should not be forgotten in the cleaning process, but the dirt that is removed should be kept well away from the paper, which could be protected by a clean piece of white paper held by drawing-pins. A vacuum cleaner with a special narrow nozzle is useful for removing loose dirt from the inside. When the case is clean, it can be examined for woodworm, and a good woodworm-killing solution applied to the affected parts. Any portions of the case that are badly eaten should be replaced, trying as far as possible to use old wood that matches the original.

If any parts of the case are damaged, they should be replaced with old but sound wood. If veneer is missing, it is best replaced by old

Left: An Ingraham 'Oak' as found. Its side wings are missing; the mainspring has broken and spread into the bottom of the case. Right: A Brewster & Ingrahams OG which was damaged by fire. The dial has been restored, and some work has been done on the case.

veneer which can often be salvaged from old items of furniture. It may pay to wait a little until a really suitable piece of veneer can be obtained rather than do the job in a hurry with whatever happens to be available. Professionals use the old-fashioned Scotch glue for veneering, for when it is dry it can be softened by the application of a warm iron if the position of the veneer needs adjusting slightly.

The pulleys on OG and column clocks should be inspected to make sure that they run freely and are not damaged. If a pulley is damaged, it should be replaced, and it is not very difficult to make one out of a piece of hard wood on the lathe using a metal-turning graver rather than a wood-turning chisel. Each pulley rides on a wire which can be pulled out lengthwise from the back of the case, and if necessary a little of the wood can be cut away to let the pliers get a grip on the wire. If the wire is very rusty, it should be replaced.

The pulleys should be covered with pieces of wood which are

An E. N. Welch Beehive as found.

fastened by nails going into the top of the case. These pieces are hollowed on the inside to allow the pulley to turn. There will usually be marks on the top of the case showing where the cover has been and giving a clue to its size. The pulley-covers not only protect the pulleys but prevent dirt from entering the case and interfering with the movement.

When the case has been cleaned and repaired and the veneer replaced, it should be polished with wax polish only. Repeated applications and plenty of rubbing will bring up a finish that shows off the beauty of the wood. The aim should be restoration, and the temptation to try to improve on the original design should be resisted. Finials should be matched as far as possible to the original using the various reference-books as a guide. A few years ago a fashion started for finishing American clocks with brightly coloured paint, but that was merely an attempt to make people interested in something which at the time was not in great demand. A great deal of work is necessary to remove the paint from one of these clocks and restore the case to its proper finish, so such a clock should be avoided in favour of a specimen that might be in worse condition but more straightforward to restore. Never finish a case with varnish stain!

If the case is decorated with gilding, such as on the capitals of the eight-day or thirty-hour column type, it is better to work on this with gold size and powder rather than buying ready mixed gold paint. There are now gilding-finishes available which have a wax basis and can be burnished after application. These are applied over a coating of a special sealer which facilitates the application of the wax.

If a tablet is damaged, it is possible to apply a little artist's oil-paint to cover the empty spaces, provided that the original design has not become flaky. If a tablet is broken, missing or practically illegible, it is possible to create one's own if one has a certain amount of skill in drawing and painting. The design is drawn actual size on tracing-paper and coloured. It is then laid face downward on a white sheet of paper so that the design shows through, and the glass laid on it with the inside upwards. Firstly the black lines are put in with a pen and black drawing-ink and then the highlights in white paint. The rest of the design is then filled in with colour using artist's oil-paint and tracing from the design below the glass. Any spaces to be gilded are left clear and covered with gold size, after which the gold powder can be carefully applied with cotton wool or velvet. When the work is dry (and it may take a day or two), the glass should be held up to the light

A selection of spare dials for late-nineteenth-century American clocks. No winding-holes have yet been drilled.

and any places where the paint has not been applied or has been applied too thinly can be touched up. After a week or two the rear of the painting can be protected with artist's varnish.

It is now possible to buy new tablets ready made, and a number of different designs are offered. Unless the collector has real skill in drawing and painting or knows someone who is gifted in this way, the ready-made replacements are the most satisfactory way of completing the job.

THE DIAL

The dial is the most noticeable part of the clock, and therefore its appearance is most important. It must be stressed that a collector should do his own dial work only if he is very skilled with pen and brush. This is particularly important in the case of the early American clocks such as the long-case and Banjo types. Even the cheaper models will not look right unless the dials have been restored to the same design as the originals.

Some of the earlier OGs and mantel clocks had wooden dials which were made of thin wood which can be brittle and were covered with a white paint which has now probably changed to a yellow or brown shade. A further feature at this period was the placing of the maker's name on the dial, and the collets for the winding-holes were very thick. If the dial has split, it should be carefully glued and the excess glue wiped away with a damp cloth. The joint should then be dried and the dial placed figures-downwards until it is hard. A heavy weight and some rubber bands (not too strong) will help to keep it in position.

Cleaning such a dial can be done with white spirit, but a very small area should be done at a time to ensure that the paint does not dissolve. If the paint does dissolve, a damp cloth with a little soap applied can also be tried, doing only a small area at a time to see the effect. Figures can be touched up with a camel-hair brush and the type of enamel that is used for modelling. The serifs on the figures are best put in with a pen and drawing-ink. It should be noted that the serifs form part of a circle and are not straight lines.

If the dial is a zinc one, which is the commonest type, white spirit can be used for cleaning, and only a small area is done at a time. Chipped portions of the dial can be made up with artist's white paint to which a tiny trace of yellow or black has been added to produce a

Setting out a new dial.

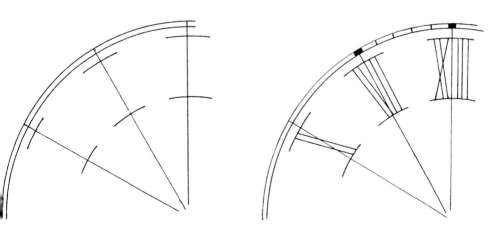

colour that matches the present state of the dial. The brass dial-collets should be removed before the dial is dealt with, and they should be cleaned and polished before replacement. The figures and minute-marks should be retouched with a pen and drawing-ink where necessary, and if large portions of the minute-track need replacing, a pen-compass using drawing-ink will do the job neatly and quickly. The dial should be secured to the bench by several drawing-pins placed round the edge and the centre found by trial and error before the pen is allowed to touch the dial. The holes in the dial centres are not always precisely located.

If a dial is so damaged that it cannot be easily restored, it must be cleaned off with abrasive paper and entirely repainted. Before removing the paint, make a drawing which shows the depth of the minute-track, the distance of the figures from the latter, the length of the figures and the length of the serifs. There is no need to finish the drawing in detail, but the dimensions are important.

If the dial has been lost, a replacement can be made using tinplate. A rectangular can is a source of supply, the sheet being cut out by shears, and then the edges must be turned as a safety precaution because the edge of a sheet of tinplate can cause a nasty cut. Allow for the turning when cutting the piece out. A round-faced hammer is used for smoothing out the dents and turning the edges.

The new dialplate has a hole made in the centre for the hand-arbors, and this can be opened with a broach as necessary. With the movement in position in the case, a spot of paint is put on the end of each winding-square and the dial placed in its correct position. When it has been finally adjusted, it is pressed slightly inwards until it touches the winding-squares and then removed. The position of the holes should be indicated by the spot of paint on the back, and the holes are then drilled and gradually opened by a broach, with adjustments being made by a rat-tail file as necessary. When the holes are the correct size, they should be smoothed and all swarf removed, after which the dial can be painted. The holes for the screws fastening the dial to the case should be made at this stage.

The dial can be rubbed with abrasive paper to give a surface for the paint to bite, and it is then cleaned with steel wool and white spirit. Household white-undercoat paint is used for the ground and is applied in several coats, the brush strokes for each coat being applied at right angles to the previous one and rubbing down done between coats if thought desirable. When a smooth, consistent surface has been produced, the figures can be added.

The layout of the figures can best be planned by looking for a photograph of a similar clock in one of the reference-books. The dial should be fixed to the bench by drawing-pins, and with a pencil-compass the circles for the minute-track and the circles marking the inner and outer side of the figures can be put in. In the latter case the circle does not have to be complete. A protractor is used to mark the twelve positions for the figures, and faint radial-lines can be drawn in with a soft pencil to show the centre line of each figure. The figures can then be lightly sketched in with a soft pencil, remembering that the centre line of each figure sometimes comes on a stroke and sometimes between strokes, e.g. the stroke representing figure I is on the centre line, while the centre line of II passes midway between the strokes. VI to XII all have their own particular position which should be studied from an existing dial.

The minute-marks are worked out by a protractor and then stepped off all round by dividers, watching carefully for accumulated errors. The design on which the dial is being based should be studied for noting whether the five-minute marks differ from the rest or only the quarter-hour marks.

When the pencil-sketch looks correct, the ink-compass should be used to put in the serifs and the minute-track, working from the inside and making each circle larger. All figures have serifs inside and outside where strokes or crosses are used, but the V does not have a serif on its point. The length of the serifs should be carefully watched. When laying out the dial, study particularly which strokes are thin and which are thick. If one is wrong, it will stand out and spoil the whole effect.

The strokes making up the figures can be added in drawing-ink with a pen and the strokes for the minutes inked in. To avoid smudging work already done, the ink can be applied to XI, XII and I first, then X and II and so on, doing the accompanying minutes at the same time. Alternatively the dial can be released from its drawing-pins and the figure at the bottom with the adjacent minutes done, after which the dial is gradually turned so that a new figure is continually taking up the bottom position. When all the ink is dry, slight corrections can be made with the blade of a very sharp penknife, and any unwanted pencil lines can be rubbed out.

Where glasses are held by bezels, these should be highly polished. Lacquer can be applied afterwards to protect the surface of the metal.

'ST' hands for Seth Thomas clocks.

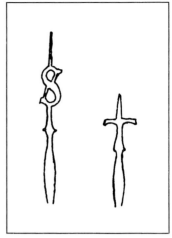

THE HANDS

New hands of various designs can now be obtained from material-dealers, but if it is desired to make one's own, it can be done from an old piece of clock mainspring which has been softened by bringing to red heat and allowing to cool. The surface is covered with layout blue and the design scratched in with a sharp steel point. The minute-hand should reach to the middle of the minute-track, and the hour-hand should come just over the serifs on the inner side of the hour-figures. The hands are cut out roughly with shears and then brought to size with a file, holding the strip of steel in the vice with clams and allowing only the minimum amount of metal to protrude. This means that the hand will constantly be re-positioned in the vice as the work proceeds. The minute-hand has a square or rectangular hole in the centre to fit its arbor, and this should be made to an accurate fit by drilling a small hole and opening it out by a square file. The hole is usually at right angles to the centre line of the hand, but it is as well to check the position of the arbor on striking-clocks so that the hand will point exactly to XII when the strike is released.

When all the cutting has been done and the edges cleaned, the face and back of the hand should be smoothed with abrasive paper held round a cork cut in half using the flat side downwards. After the surface has been finished, the hands can be blued on a brass plate over a gas flame or spirit-lamp and then quenched in oil.

The collet holding the minute-hand should be made of brass and highly polished. Many clocks are seen where the pin securing the collet has made a groove in it, but this is incorrect, and the collet should be smooth. American collets in various sizes can now be obtained from material-dealers. The tapered pin holding the collet should be cut off at each end so that it is only slightly longer than the diameter of the collet. Not only does this look neater but the pin is less

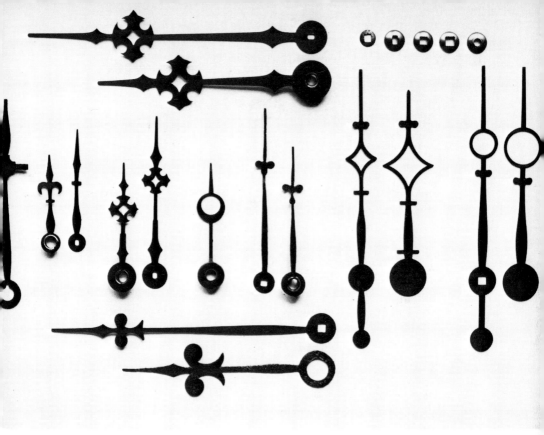

Above: A selection of hands. Top and bottom, for 12-inch dials; extreme left, an hour-hand for a Seth Thomas clock (letter T); centre, hands for various mantel clocks; right, new hands for wooden-movement shelf clocks; above, a selection of modern hand-collets. Below: A pair of Seth Thomas Cottage clocks showing the 'ST' hands.

likely to bend when it is being removed by pliers.

After the movement has been replaced in the case, and the dial and hands are on, the door with its tablet can be put back and the hinges and fastener should be polished bright.

THE LABEL

In many instances the name of the model is printed on a separate label stuck on the back of the case. As these labels are unprotected, they often get very dry and may become wholly or partially detached from the wood. Such a label greatly adds to the interest of the clock, and it can sometimes be dealt with by laying a piece of clean damp rag over it and waiting until it can be entirely removed. After removal, the label, or what is left of it, should be laid face downwards on a piece of clean paper and allowed to become perfectly dry. Any kinks or folds should be delicately removed with round-ended tweezers. When the label is dry, it can be turned right-way up and a tracing made with drawing-ink. If the label is reasonably complete, it is not too much trouble to draw in the missing letters in the same style. If a great deal of the label is missing, the task becomes more difficult, but the discolouration on the case will often indicate the size of the label to start with, and by consulting old catalogues or looking for clocks of a similar type in antique markets, salerooms etc, it should be possible to reconstruct the missing wording. After the tracing is finished, a photocopy of it should be made and stuck on the back of the clock, while the original label should be preserved from further harm in a transparent envelope which should be kept inside the clock.

In order to perform this task successfully, a certain amount of skill in drawing is necessary, and if a clock-owner feels that he is not capable of the task, it should be entrusted to someone else. The main interest in collecting clocks is to be able to tell one's friends something about their history, and any fact which gives some information on the story of a particular clock is worth recording. It also helps to increase the value if one wishes to sell. Repair-dates scribbled on the back of the dial or on the case sometimes help to give a clue to the clock's history.

This label problem will be found at its worst on some of the Waterbury clocks made about 1874 or just after, that allow the hands to be turned backwards. The paper pasted to the back of the case outside is very much larger than the labels which carry only the name of the model, and the typeface giving the information about the striking is in small letters that may be difficult to trace. With the aid of a magnifying-glass and a suitable mapping-pen, the job can be done, but it is time-consuming, and frequent rest-periods should also be taken to ease the tension in the arm. A large paper such as this is often best left in position and the tracing made thus. If the paper is nearly off anyway, then it can be removed with care by soaking and preserved in an envelope as mentioned above. Papers *in situ* can be preserved by spray lacquer after the projecting corners have been smoothed out and fastened. Take the problem to your local art-shop and ask advice on the brand to use.

A reproduction of the Briggs rotary-pendulum clock, by T. Bauerle & Söhne, St Georgen, in the Black Forest.

CLOCK SOCIETIES

Collecting, not only clocks but other things, seems to have increased in the years since 1945. When people have the same interest, they want to get together and discuss their hobby, and the next step is to form societies to further their aims and bring in new enthusiasts from a wider field. The USA can claim the first society for clock-collectors (1943), although in its early days the main interest was in watches rather than clocks. This was the National Association of Watch and Clock Collectors (notice that watch is mentioned first in the title) which now has about 33,000 members not only in the USA but in other parts of the world as well.

The Society publishes its Bulletin six times a year and includes many articles on clocks and watches, especially American ones. Another regular publication is the *Mart*, in which members advertise their wants by small advertisements and also advertise items they have for sale. The Trade is represented by booksellers and material-dealers, the latter offering parts, movements, kits for the construction of reproductions and in many instances complete clocks. During the last few years there have been numerous advertisements for old clocks of the American type made in Japan which are now being sent to the USA and disposed of by the crateful. Members are protected by the rule that no one is allowed to advertise unless he has been a member for at least six months, and in addition the advertiser's membership number has to appear in the advertisement. In order to avoid legal complications, only members resident in the USA are allowed to advertise items for sale.

Supplements to the Bulletin are published approximately once per year, and past supplements have dealt with Eli Terry (2), Welch, Spring & Co, Edward Howard, Connecticut clocks 1790–1850, a survey of the American spring-driven clock, etc. The supplements are printed in the same format as the Bulletin.

The Society holds frequent conventions in various American cities which are organized by the local Chapters, of which there are now more than a hundred. The Chapters also organize regular meetings where talks on various horological subjects are given. The Society's services include a lending library, and slide and tape material is available on loan to the Chapters only. While membership of the Society usually involves only the receipt of the Bulletin when the member is resident outside the USA, Chapters have been formed in Japan, Australia and England to organize lectures and get members acquainted with each other. Membership currently costs $20 per year, and full details can be obtained from Headquarters at PO Box 33, Columbia, Pennsylvania 17512, USA.

The American Clock and Watch Museum at Bristol, Connecticut, encourages the public to become members of the museum and, as well as offering its publications to members at reduced prices, publishes a magazine entitled *The Timepiece Journal* which comes out annually. This contains articles of interest to collectors of American clocks and deals with such subjects as old Company records, names of models used by various factories and odd items of clock history which make very interesting reading. The present subscription is $10, and details of membership can be obtained from the Museum at 100 Maple Street, Bristol, Connecticut 06010, USA. For members of the Museum who are resident in the USA, membership offers free admission to the Museum at all times it is open, and a discount on postcards, colour slides and publications sold by the Museum which it does not publish itself.

The next collectors' society to be formed was the Antiquarian Section of the British Horological Institute in 1950. The Antiquarian Horological Society came in 1953, and German collectors formed their own society, Freunde Alter Uhren, in 1960. France now has two societies, and Swiss collectors banded themselves together about the time of the opening of the new horological museum at La Chaux de Fonds in the middle 1970s.

All these societies in their early days still gave the maximum attention to the earlier clocks produced by masters in comparatively small workshops. It was the NAWCC that widened the horizon by drawing attention to the thousands of clocks that had been produced in the State of Connecticut under factory conditions and which had played an important part in developing a nation that was less than fifty years old when the mass production began. Efforts are now being made to provide an international link between all societies of clock collectors.

The American export to Britain was most effective during the years 1840–90, and following these years came the Art Nouveau and Art Deco styles. Fashions in furniture and clocks had undergone radical changes by the 1920s, and most of the imported American clocks had then had a working life that may have embraced two generations in a family. The third generation would be anxious to replace the old clocks with something modern, hence the banishment to the attics and woodsheds. A number of clocks were sold and were frequently seen in secondhand shops or places such as the Caledonian Market in North London, and were usually in a pitiful state of repair. During the 1930s the usual price for an OG was about 5 shillings (25p), and a Sharp Gothic could be obtained for 2 shillings (10p), while the smaller alarms and timepieces could be obtained for 1s 6d (7½p). A direct conversion of the old currency into new does not really give a correct impression of the value of money in those times, but the prices were very low. The clocks were considered ugly, and professional clockmakers were unwilling to repair them.

While American collectors were taking a keen interest in the products of their own country, British collectors did not become aware of the possibilities of American clocks until the 1970s. During the previous decade, an OG was seen at a jumble sale priced at 2 shillings (10p), a small timepiece for 3d (1½p) and a 12-inch wall-dial by Ansonia for 6d (2½p). With the rise in prices of all kinds of clock since 1970, collectors have turned their attention to the simpler types, and now the American clock is well established in the antiques business and reaches prices undreamed-of ten years ago.

Economic reasons are not the only ones for the changed attitude. In the very early days of collecting, few collectors understood anything about the movements of their clocks, but today great interest is taken in the technical aspect of the subject and the design of the various movements. Many collectors undertake the repair and restoration of the clocks they acquire, and this activity greatly adds to the interest. One advantage from the collector's point of view is that most of the clocks, although needing drastic repairs, have not been tampered with to increase their value, as often happens to more expensive clocks. One does see the clock that has suffered at the hands of an amateur repairer who was more concerned with making the clock tell the time than trying to pass it off as something else, but such things are luckily rare.

The problem that has confronted British collectors in the past about clocks that have been tampered with has also been present in America among the more expensive clocks such as the long-case and particularly the Banjo types. As early as 1949 the Bulletin of the

NAWCC contained an article entitled 'Simon Willard Never . . .' which listed a number of features of Banjo clocks which were quite often seen and yet were never used on genuine Willard examples. The list included such items as wrong pictures on the lower tablet, wrong dials, wrong methods of fastening doors and movements to the case, names on dials and movement and many others.

STUDYING CLOCKS

The best way to study clocks is to see as many of them as possible. This can be done in museums, antique-shops, sale-rooms etc, and a careful note of all features should be taken such as the name of the maker, type of movement, condition of dial, case and hands and so on. In this way the collector will build up knowledge of what the average American clock looks like and will learn to recognize such features as the special 'ST' hands used by Seth Thomas and the solid scapewheels used by the Forestville Manufacturing Company and E. N. Welch. He will also get an idea of what is being asked for certain examples in certain condition. Identification can be helped by consulting the reprints of the manufacturers' catalogues which are listed in the bibliography.

The specimens to be found in museums are usually in much better condition than those in circulation. In America there is the American Clock and Watch Museum at Bristol, Connecticut, the Museum of the NAWCC at Columbia, Pennsylvania, which is open to the public, the Smithsonian Institution at Washington DC and the Seth Atwood Collection at Rockford, Illinois, some 80 miles west of Chicago. The old Sturbridge Village in Massachusetts includes a number of American clocks in its collection, as does the Henry Ford Museum at Dearborn, Michigan.

There are also some American clocks in the Illinois State Museum at Springfield. The types represented are long-case, Pillar-and-Scroll, Banjo, Acorn with reversed fusees and Wagon-Spring. Unusual items include Briggs Rotary, Columbus, Plato and a gravity model by Ansonia.

California has the W. Barclay Stephens Collection at San Francisco, and a collection is now on view in Hawaii. Whenever one is in a strange town, it is always a good plan to visit the local museum. While there may not necessarily be a clock collection as such, there might be the odd clock present.

Left: A reproduction Plato clock – patent of E. L. Fitch, made by Karl Lauffer Uhrenfabrik GMBH, Schwenningen, Black Forest. Right: A reproduction Ignatz clock – A. C. Clausen, by Gebrüder Staiger, St Georgen, Black Forest.

A reproduction of Dungan's Mouse clock.

When Europe is considered, the search for museums containing American clocks is much more difficult. The Students' Room at the British Museum contains a Wagon-Spring and an Acorn, but admission to this room has to be specially applied for. The Victoria and Albert Museum has a long-case clock by Mitchell and Mott, New York, and this will show that clocks in both countries were at that time very similar except for the American tendency to use more inlay for decoration.

The American Museum at Bath is disappointing from a horological point of view, although the rest of the collection is extremely interesting and well worth a visit. A Banjo clock is displayed in one of the rooms and a lantern clock in another, but examples of the many products of the Connecticut factories are lacking.

Perhaps the largest collection of American clocks to be seen in Britain is in the museum at Kirkstall Abbey near Leeds, West

Yorkshire. In this museum an old street has been re-created with various shops including typical merchandise inside them, and the clockmaker's shop contains a wealth of material including British, German and American clocks. There is an eight-day OOG, an eight-day Sharp Gothic with alarm, Sharp Gothic and Cottage timepieces, an Ansonia striking-movement in a Royal Bonn porcelain case, a Jerome timepiece with dummy mercury pendulum and an Ansonia wall regulator. Seth Thomas is represented by two examples, a calendar clock and an 'Oak' fitted with Wood's Patent Alarm. Many of these clocks are inside the shop and cannot be clearly seen from outside, but permission to see them may be granted on written application. In another part of the museum is a Baird Advertising Clock.

A wooden movement is displayed in the Willis Museum at Basingstoke, Hampshire, and there are two more in the Pinto collection of wooden bygones in the City Art Gallery in Birmingham. The eight-day Column clock can be found at Lewes, Sussex (Barbican House Museum) and at Leicester (Newarke Houses Museum), although the clock is in store at the time of writing. This museum contains a large collection of Leicestershire clocks and in addition displays the workshop of the Deacon family of Barton in the Beans, a village some miles away. The workshop includes a variety of clocks left for repair, as well as the tools, and the clocks include a Chauncey Jerome Beehive with fusees and a clock from the Portsoken Manufacturing Company with the Holloway stamp on the rear.

The collection of the Welsh Folk Museum at St Fagans near Cardiff includes an eight-day Sharp Gothic with strike and alarm by Jerome & Co and another alarm by the same maker. The firm has also contributed an OG, but unfortunately the collection is in store at the time of writing.

OGs can be found at Ilfracombe Museum, Tiverton Castle, Tiverton Museum, the Museum of the History of Science at Oxford and the Museum of Lakeland Life at Kendal, Cumbria. The latter museum also has a Newhaven eight-day mantel clock with Kroeber pendulum.

There is little to report from the Continent, but the Netherlands Clock Museum at Schoonhoven near Gouda possesses a Silas Hoadley 'Upside Down' movement and an unusual balance-movement by Charles Kirke with two scapewheels. The German Clock Museum at Furtwangen includes an Ansonia mantel clock, a

'Marine or Locomotive' clock and a beautiful early example of a German OG which still shows the craftsmanship of the workshop although based on a factory design. The Abeler Museum in Wuppertal contains an Ansonia Sharp Gothic striking-clock with alarm.

It is easier to see American clocks in antique-shops and markets in Britain than in museums. Most cathedral cities have a number of antique-shops, and antique-markets are now very fashionable. In London is the famous Bermondsey market which operates on Fridays, and surrounding the market territory proper are a number of side streets where there are warehouses offering antiques for sale. The district round Islington Green in North London has a large number of antique-shops, and there are now three areas that can be considered antique-markets contiguous with them. Kings Road, Chelsea, also has a number of antique-shops. In the provinces, there is the area in Brighton known as 'The Lanes' and antique-markets in Lewes and Chichester, to select two towns at random, and further north Warwick and Keighley also possess antique-markets, as well as many other towns too numerous to mention. Great Yarmouth is a good spot in East Anglia, as well as some of the smaller towns in the area. Most seaside towns have an area devoted to antique-shops, however small. Apart from towns, many antique-shops have been established along main roads in various parts of the country.

REPRODUCTIONS

In recent years the practice of creating reproductions of older types has become very much more prevalent. For reproductions of American clocks the best place to seek them is naturally America itself, but there is one outstanding exception to the rule. This is a reproduction Banjo clock by Biddle & Mumford (Gears) Ltd of 36–42 Clerkenwell Road, London. The clock is close to its prototype in outline and size and can be fitted with a weight-driven or an electric movement as desired. The weight-movement is based on the original design and has the pendulum just behind the dial, with the winding-hole at the two o'clock position. Clocks with the electric movement do not have the winding-hole in the dial. The clock is much more convincing than the reproduction Banjos that were being made by American factories in the early years of the century.

Clock Trade Enterprises of Bronxville, New York, have supplied several reproduction clocks in the last few years, including the Columbus, Plato, Ignatz and Briggs Rotary. The latter in particular is a very fine clock, standing on a base of African wood, and is an improvement on its predecessor in that it goes for eight days on a winding instead of two. No fewer than eight arbors are required in the train. These clocks have been made in the Black Forest by T. Bauerle & Söhne of St Georgen.

The Mouse clock is a reproduction of one of the unusual ideas that come on the market from time to time. The original dates from 1911, and the time is shown by a mouse that slowly climbs a scale of hours indicating the time by the tip of its nose. The scale is calibrated from one to one, and when the mouse reaches the top, the clock strikes one and the mouse runs down to the bottom again. The Ignatz keeps time just as crazily as its predecessor, but the Plato has a seven-jewel eight-day movement that is claimed to be an improvement on the original.

The Howard Company, formerly of Boston but now in Waltham, Massachusetts, has produced a new model of the 'Figure Eight Banjo', 2 ft 9 inches long with an 8-inch dial. The series is limited to a thousand pieces, and the new clock differs from the old in having a pendulum-rod made of Invar to compensate for changes in temperature.

Various firms are offering reproduction clocks in a series, most of which use the same movement. One of the producers advertises that his movement is based on the Ansonia movement of 1882. Not only American models such as the Schoolhouse and the Banjo are included but also German types such as the Berliner and the small spring-driven version of the Vienna Regulator. The stress seems to be on wall clocks in accordance with the present-day fashion of eliminating mantelpieces from the home. One exception to this rule is the clock in the shape of a violin that was made by Seth Thomas, and there is another model based on the Welch, Spring & Co mantel clock Parepa of 1877.

A replica of the Patti Regulator introduced by Welch, Spring & Co in 1882–4 follows the original very closely but can be supplied with a movement having Westminster chimes if desired. This feature was not included by the original makers and weakens the case for acquiring a reproduction. A replica of an Eli Terry Pillar and Scroll conforms very closely to the shape of the original but has the plates of the movement and the dial made of Plexiglass so that the wheels can

Above: A reproduction of Howard's 'Figure of Eight' Banjo by the Howard Clock Company.

Right: A reproduction Banjo clock by Biddle & Mumford (Gears) Ltd, London.

be seen. Reproduction clocks do not always have the dials in the correct style, nor do the standard movements that are fitted in many instances have the winding-squares in the same position as on the original clocks.

The Ansonia 'Swinger' has also been included in the reproductions of recent years and can be supplied with either a flat or a hemispherical dial.

KITS AND MATERIAL

Not only reproductions of complete clocks are being offered in America but also kits for constructing one's own clock. A favourite model is the Schoolhouse clock with the day of the month shown outside the hour-figures. A kit for the case of a Terry-type Pillar-and-Scroll clock can be supplied but has an eight-day half-hour strike-movement which is spring-driven. With the kit comes a reproduction label to stick in the back of the case. Many kits are available for constructing one's own long-case clock, but there is usually no attempt to imitate an old model in these but rather to base the design on the type of clock that was being made at the turn of the century, usually incorporating quarter-chimes and having the pendulum and weights visible.

For enthusiasts who prefer to do their own construction and repairs, there is a wide selection of material offered by various firms in the USA. Sets of pallets are made with the operative part left straight so that they can be bent to the shape necessary for a particular clock, or pallets can be supplied with the ends already bent but requiring all the components to be assembled and adjusted. A new idea is offered by material-dealers for replacing broken or worn pivots. An assortment of short sections of arbor with a pivot on one end is supplied, and the opposite end of the arbor is drilled to about half its length. The arbor of the clock with the broken pivot is trimmed to fit the drilled portion tightly, and then the pivot is dressed to correct size. It is claimed that the work can be done by hand, using a stone if a lathe is not available.

A number of pendulum-bobs which are copies of those used by factories in the nineteenth century are also available. They range from simple circular ones with an embossed design to the very

A reproduction Girandole by Elmer Stennes.

elaborate type that were used when the glass was usually left plain and the decorated pendulum-bob took the place of the painted tablet as a decoration for the clock. Complete pendulums of the imitation mercury and gridiron types are also sold. The ordinary type of bob with a loop for hanging on the pendulum-wire is available in two sizes, one for eight-day clocks and one for thirty-hour clocks. The imitation marble clocks and others using a rear pendulum-movement usually had the opening in the back of the case covered by a circular iron plate. These plates are now available from material-dealers once again. Veneer can be supplied for case-repairs, and splats and feet for Empire-style cases are also available. Hands and dials in old styles are also made, and basic materials such as keys, mainsprings and taper-pins are supplied.

For those people who wish to design and build their own cases, movements are available. Many are adaptable to a number of designs, but there are two in particular that should be mentioned. A replica of the British-type long-case movement with solid plates and rack-strike that was used by many American clockmakers has been put on the market, and also a small and a large calendar-movement such as was used in the Ithaca calendar clocks.

A new movement has been designed for Oaks and similar clocks, with a front pendulum that is suspended on a special bracket above the top of the movement instead of from a point near the centre. The plates are finished in the modern style, and the springs are contained in barrels instead of being open. The barrels are of the modern detachable kind that can be removed from the clock without having to take the whole movement to pieces. Striking is on the rack system instead of the count-wheel, and half-hours are struck. When the movement is in the case, it cannot be seen, but the purist might object to the fact that, the pendulum being longer than on the old clocks, the tick would be a little slower. The same movement is sold suitable for 13-inch and 17-inch pendulums which allows it to be used in Schoolhouse and other types of wall clock. In all three sizes the hammer is below.

A series of drawings of various American movements is being issued by a publisher in America, and other firms issue plans of clocks to be made, including a shelf clock of the taller type that followed Terry's Pillar-and-Scroll design. The latter plans include not only the case but also the individual parts of the wooden-wheeled movement.

Services are offered, such as tablets with reverse paintings incorporating the purchaser's own design, and repairers will undertake restoration of movements, even those with wooden wheels.

The collector in Britain is well provided with material and services for restoring British clocks, but the position is naturally not so favourable where American clocks are concerned. Luckily, however, a number of the firms that offer British and Continental material now supply American parts and accessories such as pendulum-bobs, pendulum-wires, hands, sets of pallets, boxes of American bushes and keys. The special cord for OGs has been out of stock for some time, but there are hopes that it will be available again. It is now possible to purchase glass tablets for OG and smaller clocks decorated in the traditional style, and a fair selection is being offered.

Complete clocks of the American type are not so common in Britain, but the Briggs Rotary is on sale, and a firm is making reproductions of Ansonia mantel clocks with a glass door covering the whole front and the Ansonia Trade Mark on the dial. The style is roughly that of the 1880s, and the clock would be classified as a kitchen clock.

The periodicals offered by the various Societies are a good source of information on where to obtain clocks both antique and repro-duction and also the various items of material together with the services offered. Other periodicals are issued: in America there is *The American Horologist and Jeweler* and two new ones called *Clockwise* and the *Horological Times*. In Britain the *Horological Journal* and *Antiquarian Horology* both contain advertisements for booksellers and material-dealers, but the magazine *Clocks* contains a wider selection of suppliers who cater more for amateurs and collectors.

Bibliography

In order to derive the most from the hobby of clock-collecting, it is necessary to know as much as possible about the clocks that one collects. The following selection of books should be of use in building up background knowledge for the collector, as well as filling in details of makers and constructional features. All the books, with the exception of two, are published in America but often feature in the catalogues of specialist horological booksellers in Britain.

The old manufacturers' catalogues especially are of great value. The drawings in them usually give a very good idea of what a certain model looks like, and in the case of those published by the American Clock and Watch Museum, the dates at which a certain model was discontinued are often shown. Many of the catalogues are now out of print, and while most of the books are still current at the time of writing (1980), stocks may be running low. The specialist booksellers will probably be able to supply secondhand copies of both books and catalogues if new ones are not available. While some of the books mentioned are quite old, they have been reprinted by photographic methods in recent years.

Old numbers of the Bulletin of the NAWCC are being reprinted to be offered to new members of the Society and contain a great variety of material. It is undoubtedly the leading periodical in which to find information on American clocks. The book on Jesse Coleman also contains a wealth of American material. Back numbers of British antique-journals deal with American subjects only in rare cases, but there is always the chance that old copies of American antique-magazines can be found in secondhand-booksellers' shops and it pays to be always on the alert.

The addresses of horological booksellers in Britain can be found in the advertisement columns of such periodicals as the *Horological Journal, Antiquarian Horology* and *Clocks*. The *Mart* of the NAWCC will give similar addresses in the USA and Canada.

Following the title of each book in the list are a few comments on the type of material the book deals with. A number of them are concerned mainly with the earlier periods of clock making such as are covered by Chapter I of the present work, and the clocks are therefore less accessible to British readers. The latter will naturally be more concerned with the factory-made clocks that were exported to Britain and which are therefore more available as items for collection. This should not deter them from making a study of the older periods, however, for the history of clockmaking in America is a fascinating story, and it adds to the interest of one's collection if its background is known.

The list of books is not exhaustive, for the subject was already being written about many years ago, and many of the earlier books will now be out of print and virtually unobtainable. An attempt has been made to include titles that will be more readily available to the present-day reader. It is a comfort to know that the stock of literature is continually being augmented, for the number of people who take an interest in clocks is growing every year, and new books are frequently being published. On the other hand, the remaining clocks are less readily available for collectors, but if it is not possible to own the clocks, then the next best alternative is to read about them.

Allix, Charles. *Carriage Clocks* (Antique Collectors' Club, Wood-bridge; 400 pp, $8\frac{1}{4} \times 11$.). A history and development of the carriage clock which includes American examples.

Bailey, Chris. *Two Hundred Years of American Clocks and Watches* (Prentice Hall Inc; 254 pp, 9×11). A well-illustrated book with a number of illustrations in colour and portraits of American clockmakers. Plenty of material on the older types of clock.

Bailey, Chris. *160 Years of Seth Thomas Clocks* (Bulletin of the Connecticut Historical Society, Vol. 38, No. 3, July 1973; 10 pp text, 5 pp illustrations, B & W, 6×9.) A history of Seth Thomas and the firm he founded.

Battison, Edwin, and Kane, Patricia. *The American Clock, 1725–1865* (New York Graphic Society, Greenwich, Connecticut; 207 pp, $9\frac{3}{4} \times 10\frac{1}{4}$). The title of this book is misleading for it is in fact a catalogue in great detail of the Collection of Yale University. The stress is on long-case clocks, and illustrations of dials and movements are included, showing that the latter were often imported from Britain. Only one OG represents the brass-movement factory clocks, but some wood movements are shown and also Case-on-Case and Banjo clocks.

Chandlee E. E. *Six Quaker Clockmakers* (Historical Society of

Pennsylvania; 260 pp, 163 illustrations). Information on Pennsylvania makers.

Darnall J. V. *Restoration of Old American Wood Clocks* and *Restoration of Old American Brass Clocks* (Tampa, Florida; Paper. 28 pp, $5\frac{1}{2} \times 8\frac{1}{2}$). Down-to-earth instructions on repairing.

Distin, William H. and Bishop, Robert. *The American Clock* (E. P. Dutton & Co Inc; 359 pp, $9 \times 11\frac{1}{4}$). This book surveys the history of clockmaking in America 1723–1900, but the story is told by illustrations rather than text. A very large number of clocks are dealt with. A list of clockmakers is included and also a selection of tools. Many illustrations in colour.

Drepperd Carl W. *American Clocks and Clockmakers* (Doubleday & Co Inc: 364 pp, $5\frac{1}{2} \times 8\frac{1}{2}$). This book gives a history of the development of the American clock and includes a list of makers. Illustrations are from both photographs and reproductions from old manufacturers' catalogues.

Drost, William E. *Clocks and Watches of New Jersey* (Elizabeth, NJ; 291 pp, 7×11). A review of clockmaking in the State of New Jersey which includes a number of illustrations showing how clockmakers would cut off a piece of brass from imported movements for their own use. Aaron D. Crane and the torsional pendulum are dealt with.

Dworetsky, Lester, and Dickstein, Robert. *Horology Americana* (Roslyn Heights, NY; 222 pp, $7\frac{1}{2} \times 10$). Three hundred illustrations of antique clocks from Colonial days, including 204 in colour.

Eckhardt, George H. *Pennsylvania Clocks and Clockmakers* (Devin Adair Co; 229 pp, 7×10). Pennsylvania has a long history of horology, and this book records the many long-case clocks that were made and also discusses the influence of the many German immigrants to the State. Technical matters are also mentioned.

Eckhardt, George H. *United States Clock and Watch Patents, 1790–1890* (New York; 231 pp, $5\frac{1}{2} \times 8\frac{1}{2}$). The patents have been classified under subject, but little detail is given. It is useful when looking up American patents at the British Library. Few illustrations.

Ela, Chipman P. *The Banjo Timepiece* (Fryeburg, Maine; 200 pp, about 400 illustrations). A description of a collection of Banjo clocks which had been packed away for about forty years. The chief advantage is that restorers and fakers have had less opportunity to alter these clocks, which can be accepted as being more likely to be authentic than many examples seen.

Gibbs, James W. *Buckeye Horology* (Artcrafters Printers: 128 pp, $8\frac{1}{2} \times 11$). A review of clock- and watchmaking in Ohio. Includes patents up to 1890.

Gibbs, James W. *Dixie Clockmakers* (Pelican Publishing Co; 191 pp, 59 illustrations, $8\frac{1}{2} \times 11$). This book deals with the makers of the Southern States about whom little has been written in the past. It contains material on the clockmakers' lives as well as the clocks that they made.

Gibbs, James W. *Life and Death of the Ithaca Calendar Clock Company* (Pennsylvania; 1960. 80 pp, 6×9). A description of one of the firms making calendar clocks.

Hagans, Orville R. *The Best of Coleman, Clockmaker* (American Watchmakers' Institute Press; 536 pp, 340 illustrations, $6 \times 9\frac{1}{2}$). For nearly thirty years the late Jesse Coleman conducted a question-and-answer column in the *American Horologist and Jeweler*. The material ranged over a wide field of horology, particularly American, and a number of the articles have been reprinted here. The book is well indexed, a necessity in view of the number of subjects dealt with.

Hoopes, Penrose R. *Connecticut Clockmakers of the Eighteenth Century* (Dover Publications, New York; 182 pp, paper, 59 illustrations, $6\frac{1}{2} \times 9\frac{1}{4}$). As the title would suggest, this deals with clockmaking before the establishment of factories, but it forms a good background to what came later.

Hoopes, Penrose R. *Shop Records of Daniel Burnap, Clockmaker* (The Connecticut Historical Society; 188 pp, numerous illustrations, $7 \times 10\frac{1}{4}$). Daniel Burnap was trained by Thomas Harland and was the master of Eli Terry. Here is a record of his business transactions together with an insight into his workshop methods. Burnap was active from about 1779 to 1805 and was the most successful clockmaker in Connecticut. This period was still the era of hand-made clocks, and the book gives an insight into the work done before the factories took over.

Hudson Moore, N. *The Old Clock Book* (Tudor Publishing Co; 339 pp, 104 illustrations, $5\frac{3}{4} \times 8\frac{1}{4}$). Not only American clocks are dealt with in this book but also British ones. Lists of makers are given, and the text is mainly concerned with the period before the clock-factories were set up.

Jerome, Chauncey. *History of the American Clock Business for the last Sixty Years and the Life of Chauncey Jerome* (Adams Brown; 59 pp, 6×9). Jerome played an important part in the establishment of the Connecticut export trade. His reminiscences do not always tally with the research of other writers, but this is nevertheless a most important book.

Milham, Willis I. *Time and Timekeepers* (Macmillan; 8vo, 616 pp, 339 illustrations). A general review on the history of time measurement but with stress on American clocks.

Milham, Willis I. *The Columbus Clock* (New York, 1945; 34 pp, $6 \times 9\frac{1}{4}$, paper). The reproduction clocks sold at the World's Fair in 1893.

Miller, Andrew and Dalia, *Survey of American Calendar Clocks* (Antiquitat, Elgin, Illinois; 160 pp, 9×12, 520 illustrations). Many different types of calendar clock are discussed, covering a large number of firms. Patent specifications are included and many close-ups of mechanisms.

Mussey, Barrows. *Young Father Time* (The Newcomen Society; 44 pp, $6\frac{1}{4} \times 9\frac{1}{4}$, 24 illustrations). A biography of Eli Terry with illustrations of some of his early clocks.

Mussey, Barrows and Canedy, Ruth Mary. *Terry Clock Chronology* (Charles Terry Treadway, Bristol; 28 pp, paper, $8\frac{1}{2} \times 11$). A collection of documentary references to material relating to Eli Terry sr and jr.

Osborn, N. G. (ed). *History of Connecticut* (States History Co, New York, 1925, Vol. IV. The section on clockmaking occupies pp. 33–56 and mentions a number of factories.

Palmer, Brooks. *The Book of American Clocks* (Macmillan; 318 pp, 312 illustrations $7\frac{3}{4} \times 10\frac{1}{2}$). One of the best-known books on collecting American clocks. The illustrations form the bulk of the work, and many different types of clock are dealt with. The list of makers is extremely useful.

Palmer, Brooks. *A Treasury of American Clocks* (Macmillan; 371 pp, 558 illustrations, $7\frac{3}{4} \times 10\frac{1}{2}$). This book forms an excellent companion to the previous one. The illustrations are in groups, such as OG Wagon Spring, Beehive etc, and the list of makers, which extends and corrects the one in the previous volume, is nearly fifty pages long. The material ranges from early long-case clocks to drum-alarms.

Parsons, Charles S. *New Hampshire Clocks and Clockmakers* (Adams Brown; 356 pp, 551 illustrations, $9 \times 11\frac{1}{4}$). This book is particularly important for its detailed studies of both wooden and brass movements. In particular the shape of the plates of the New Hampshire Mirror clocks show the drastic shortage of metal that the clockmakers of the early-nineteenth century had to cope with. Particularly interesting for the technically minded reader.

Roberts, Kenneth D. *The Contributions of Joseph Ives to Connecticut Clock Technology* (American Clock and Watch Museum; 338 pp, profusely illustrated, $8\frac{3}{4} \times 11\frac{1}{4}$). This is the finest book that has been written on the growth of the factory system in Connecticut. As well as the theme indicated by the title, many other subjects are dealt with, and all information is carefully documented. The illustrations are large and clear and include such subjects as a very early OG with solid wheels, clock papers, wagon-spring movements, early reversed fusees etc, and a number of patent specifications are reproduced such as Noble Jerome's striking mechanism, Ives's wagon spring, reversed fusees, Ives's tinplate movement and others. This is a book for the really serious student of American horological history.

Roberts, Kenneth D. *Eli Terry and the Connecticut Shelf Clock* (Ken Roberts Publishing Co; 320 pp, 152 illustrations, $9 \times 11\frac{1}{4}$). Once again one can say that this is a most important book. It begins with the long-case clocks having both wooden and brass movements that Terry was used to when he began work as a clockmaker and traces the various types of wooden-movement shelf clock that he made, in many cases giving views of the wheelwork assembled with the top plate of the movement removed. The illustrations are very clear and include labels and complete clocks as well as drawings of train layouts etc. While the book is concerned mostly with wooden movements, brass movements are not forgotten. Also a book for the serious enthusiast.

Schiff, Leonard J. and Schiff, Joseph L. *Edward Payson Baird* (published by authors; 61 pp, 87 illustrations, $8\frac{1}{2} \times 11$, paper). Contains a section of the advertising clocks made by Baird together with a number of views of the Seth Thomas movements he placed in them.

Shenton, Alan and Rita. *The Price Guide to Clocks, 1840–1940* (Antique Collectors' Club, Woodbridge, Suffolk; 541 pp, profusely illustrated, $5\frac{1}{2} \times 8\frac{1}{4}$). This book deals with many clocks in the cheaper price-bracket among them being a number of American types. Drum-alarms, Fattorini alarms and the products of the British United Clock Company are dealt with, and the book gives a good general picture of what was being bought in Britain at the time when American clocks were being exported in large numbers.

Slobin, Herman. *The Florence Kroeber Story* (published by the author; 53 pp, profusely illustrated, 9×11). There is a short biography of Kroeber, and then a number of his Patent Specifications are reproduced, followed by photographs of his clocks. The earlier type of recording pendulum-bob appears in more than one illustration, but the second type is not shown, nor is there any mention of these pendulums in the text.

Willard, John Ware. *Simon Willard and his Clocks* (Dover Publications Inc; 133 pp, profusely illustrated, $6\frac{3}{4} \times 9\frac{1}{4}$, paper). The work of Simon Willard and his family is dealt with, including long-case, Banjo and Case-on-Case clocks.

Wood, Stacy B. C. jr, and Kramer, Stephen E. III. *Clockmakers of*

Lancaster County and their Clocks, 1750–1850 (Van Nostrand Reinhold; 224 pp, profusely illustrated, 9 × 11). This detailed study of clockmaking in a comparatively small area shows the influence of the German immigrants to the area. While most of the clocks were based on British models, there were differences. Generally speaking, the thirty-hour clocks were of higher quality than were being made in Britain at the time. An important feature is that many clocks are illustrated complete, and other illustrations show close-ups of dials and movements with an index to link all the photographs together. A work for the serious student of horology.

Wood, Stacy B. C. jr. *The Hoff Family: Master Clockmakers of Lancaster Borough* (Journal of the Lancaster County Historical Society, Vol. 81, 1977; 56 pp, 6 × 9). A fully documented account of one of the most well-known clockmaking families in the area. Illustrations of clocks, portraits and advertisements.

Wood, Stacy B. C. jr. *225 Years of Timepieces* (A Lancaster County Legacy, NAWCC; 84 pp, $5\frac{1}{2} \times 8\frac{1}{2}$, paper). This is a catalogue of the first annual exhibition held by the NAWCC in Columbia, Pennsylvania, 1979, recording the making of clocks and watches in Lancaster County. Illustrations include clocks, watches, advertisements and tools.

CATALOGUES

Published by the American Clock and Watch Museum, Bristol, Connecticut.

Jerome	1852	Terry Clock Co (in-	
Jerome	1853	cluding Henry Terry's	
Seth Thomas	1863	*History of the American*	
Howard	1874	*Clock Business)*	1885
Gilbert	1875	Howard (Hall	
Ansonia	1880	striking-clocks)	1888
New Haven	1880	Western Clock Co	1902
Welch	1880	Sessions Clock Co	1915
Ingraham	1880	Herschede	1923
Ingraham	1881		1923/4
			1929

Published by The Adams Brown Company, Exeter, New Hampshire.

Welch	1885	Boston Clock Co	1890
New Haven	1889/90		

Published by American Reprints Company, Ironton, Missouri.

Waterbury	1867	St Louis Clock and	
American Clock Co	1878	Silverware Co	1904
Seth Thomas	1879	Seth Thomas	1904/5
Waterbury	1881	Ansonia Crystal	
Myers, Clapp & Davis	1885/6	Regulators	1905
Becken	1896	Waterbury	1908
Ansonia	1886/7		
Prentiss Clock			
Improvement Co	1897		

Published by Arlington Book Company, Arlington, Virginia.

G. S. Lovell	1874	Howard tower clocks etc	1900
(various makers)		Howard tower clocks	1923
New Haven	1900	Seth Thomas	1909/10
Welch	1900	Chelsea Clock Co	1911
Howard	1900		

Published by Elgin Book Company, Elgin, Illinois.

Gilbert	1901/2

Appendix 1   Clock Papers

The Jerome OG paper:

'Patent Brass Clocks made and sold by Chauncey Jerome, Bristol Conn. Warranted good.

'Directions for setting the clock running and keeping it in order.

'N.B. The clock can be set running without taking off the hands or dial plate. Put the pendulum through the loop at the end of the wire at the bottom of the dial and hang it in the stud above.

'Oil the pallets or ends of the part commonly called the verge, the pin on which the verge plays, and the wire which carries the pendulum at the place where it touches the rod. One drop of oil is sufficient for the whole.

'Care should be taken not to wind the clock until the cord is put upon the pully in the partition and also on the top of the case and the weights put on. The light weight on the strike side of the clock.

'To wind up the weights put on the key with the handle down, turn towards the figure VI and turn steady until the weight is up.

'If the hands want moving, do it by means of the longest, turning it at any time forward but never backward when the clock is within fifteen minutes of striking; and in no case further than to carry the minute hand up to the figure XII.

'Directions for Regulating the Clock.

'This is done by means of a screw at the bottom of the pendulum. If the clock should go too fast lower the ball, if too slow raise it.'

Papers from inside and outside a Waterbury striking-clock which contradict each other:

Inside: 'Waterbury Clock Co. Waterbury Conn. Manufacturers of Eight Day and Thirty Hour Brass Clocks and Timepieces.

'Directions for setting the clock running and keeping it in order. The clock can be set running without taking off the hands or dial-plate. If the hands want moving do it by means of the longest, turning it at any time forward but never backward when the clock is within 15 minutes of striking and in no case farther than to carry the minute hand to the figure XII. If the clock strikes wrong it may be made to strike right by lifting a wire under the figure VII.

'Directions for regulating the clock.

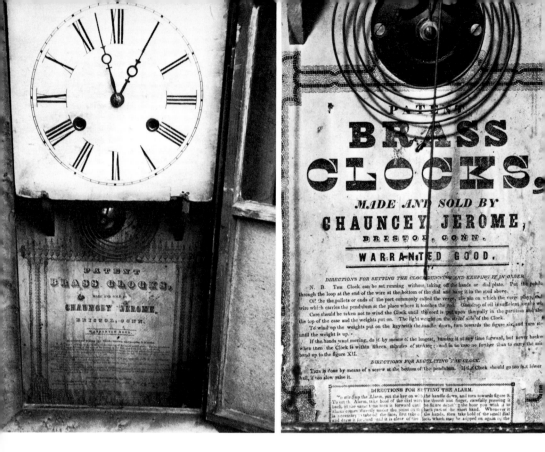

OG labels by Chauncey Jerome, pre 1845. Left: Bristol, Connecticut. Right: A different style with additional instructions for the alarm pasted below.

'This is done by means of a screw at the bottom of the pendulum. If the clock should go too fast lower the ball; if too slow raise it.'
Outside: 'Waterbury Clock Co. Waterbury Conn.

'Directions for setting the clock running and keeping it in order.

'The long hand is the minute hand, the short hand the hour hand.

'Remove the packing wire holding the pendulum rod, and hang the ball on the rod. The beat should be equal and regular, and will be so if the clock is set in a LEVEL position.

'To set the clock. – Always use the minute hand (which can be turned in either direction without injury); never turn the hour hand.

'The clock is regulated by means of a screw at the bottom of the pendulum. If the clock should go too fast lower the ball; if too slow, raise it.

'DIRECTIONS FOR SETTING ALARMS IN ALARM CLOCKS.

'Turn the alarm dial to the right till the desired hour (as indicated

The label of a Waterbury thirty-hour Cottage clock.

A Jerome & Co (New Haven Clock Company) label of the late-nineteenth century.

on the dial) lies directly beneath the hour hand; then wind the alarm.

'Directions for a striking clock.

'The clock can be made to strike to correspond with the position of the hands, by carrying the minute hand forward to the figure II, then backward to the figure VIII, and back and forth between the figures until the right hour is struck.'

Paper from a New Haven Sharp Gothic incorporating advertising material.

'Eight day and   Thirty Hour
OG and OOG with & Without alarms
 Gothic   Spring
Eight day & 30 Hour Sharp and Round top
With and without alarms
Marine Lever timepieces, for Ships, Steamboats
Locomotives and Dwellings
Octagon Eight day clocks silent and striking
for hotels, offices &c.
All warranted of the best quality
made by
New Haven Clock Co., New Haven Ct.

'Directions for regulating the clock.

'This is done by means of a screw at the bottom of the pendulum. If the clock should go too fast lower the ball, if too slow raise it. If the hands want moving do it by means of the longest, turning it at any time forward but never backward when the clock is within fifteen minutes of striking and in no case further than to carry the minute hand to the figure XII.

'If the clock should strike wrong in consequence of its running down or other accident, it may be made to strike by lifting the wire directly under the figure 7.

'Benham Steam Printer New Haven.'

Note: A paper with identical wording to the above has been found in a Sharp Gothic by the Ansonia Brass Company, Ansonia, Connecticut.

The printer is the same, and it would appear that he kept the type set up for whichever factory needed papers.

An Ansonia timepiece Sharp Gothic has been seen with instructions on the paper as on a larger clock. Timepieces usually have more abbreviated papers.

A later paper from Waterbury, c. 1900. This was in a lancet case with a movement having a rear pendulum and bell for half-hour strike.

'American Manufacture.

Enfield.

'Manufactured by Waterbury Clock Co, Waterbury Conn. USA.

47–49 Maiden Lane New York	63 Franklin Street Boston
215 W. Randolph St Chicago	144–146 Ingram St Glasgow
Jewellers Building 150	31–33 Wellington St
Post St San Francisco	East Toronto

'Directions for setting the clock running and keeping it in order.

'Remove the paper or packing wire holding the rod and hang the ball on the rod. Beware that the paper or packing wire is taken out of the clock, for if left in it is liable to get into the movement and stop the clock. The beat should be equal and regular and will be so if the clock is set in a level position. This clock is fitted with our No 30 A-2 movement, eight day spring striking the hours and half hours. To set the clock use the long or minute hand only. Never try to turn the short or hour hand. The minute hand can be turned in either direction without injury to the clock.

Left: An OG of the Forestville Clock Company, 1850s. Note the motto, 'The Union Now and Forever'. Right: A Beehive from Gilbert, of Winchester, Connecticut, possibly pre 1870.

'The clock can be made to strike to correspond with the position of the hands by carrying the minute hand forward to the figure II and then backward to the figure VIII and back and forth between these figures until the right hour is struck.

'The clock is fitted with our patent regulator whereby it can be regulated without touching the pendulum by means of the small arbor just over the figure XII. If the clock goes slow turn to the right, if fast turn to the left.

'If for any reason the clock should not regulate satisfactorily from the front, it can be regulated the same as any ordinary clock by the raising or lowering of the pendulum ball itself. Raise the ball to make the clock go faster lower it to make it go slower.

'To secure the most accurate timekeeping and the best results generally, the clock should be wound regularly once a week.'

(*Note:* The later striking-clocks by William Gilbert allowed regulation only from the dial. There was no rating-nut on the bob.)

Appendix 2 Export to Britain

The earliest distributor of American clocks in Britain was Epaphroditus Peck, who had a contract with Chauncey Jerome to dispose of the clocks that Jerome sent over. William Holloway has already been mentioned, and Brewster & Ingrahams had their own agent, Noah L. Brewster, at 13 Walbrook, London. Henry Mayhew, who wrote *London Labour and the London Poor* in the 1850s, said that American clocks were sold in 'swag shops', i.e. shops of general dealers who usually sold wholesale and were generally Jews. He mentioned the great variety of merchandise that was found in these shops. The *West Briton* of the 1840s contained an advertisement by Ramsey of Devonport offering American clocks, and in 1846 Charles Levy of Truro and Morris Hart Harris of Penzance were offering them at 17s 6d each. These were almost certainly OGs.

An advertisement has come to light from the *History, Gazetteer and Directory of Warwickshire* for 1850 showing the type of merchandise that was handled by such dealers:

Louis & Mier
Merchants and Factors.
Edgbaston Street Birmingham
and New York.
Manufacturers of jewelry, German silver, and silver plated wares, Bronzes, Papier Mâché, Importers of toys, Beads, Coral, Porcelain, Musical Boxes, Clocks, and every description of French and German merchandise; Birmingham and Sheffield Warehousemen; Depot for American clocks, Accordians, Rosewood Work Boxes, Dressing Cases, Writing Desks, Tea Chests, Backgammon boards, Telescopes, Glass Wares, Guns, Pistols &c. Perfumery, Combs, Brushes, and fancy Articles, in Great Variety.
SHIPPING ORDERS EXECUTED

Production figures are always somewhat doubtful but the following are included as an item of interest. They relate to the year 1868.

New Haven	150,000	Waterbury	50,000
E. N. Welch	100,000	Gilbert	40,000
Seth Thomas	75,000	Ansonia	10,000

Price $1–10, average $2½.

The first American firm to open an office in London was Seth Thomas in 1874, manager R. M. Marples. The address was 16 Worship Street, and two years later E. N. Welch was represented at the same address. In 1883 Seth Thomas moved to 7 Cripplegate Buildings, and in 1885 the Welch Office moved to 99 Fenchurch Street. Ansonia appointed Holloway & Co of 128/9 Minories as their agents in 1879 but in 1883 had their own office at 51 Holborn Viaduct, moving to 23 Fore Street two years later, B. M. Davies, manager. The British Jerome Company, i.e. a sales organization, opened at 58 Holborn Viaduct in 1884 and in the following year was at 99 Fenchurch Street joined by New Haven. British United established an office at 34 Farringdon Road in 1888, and William Gilbert at 99 Fenchurch Street in 1891. Jerome and New Haven moved to 7 Snow Hill in 1896, and Ingrahams began at 26 Chapel Street in 1900.

In spite of the manufacturers establishing London offices, some independent importers still remained, such as John G. Rollins & Co, Old Swan Wharf, Upper Thames Street, Thomas Greenwood & Co, importers of American clocks and watches, 55 Holborn Viaduct, and Perry & Co, also in Holborn Viaduct. These firms were gone by the end of the century.

The various offices must have been persuasive, for even Harrods showed American clocks in their catalogue of 1895. Business was not done entirely in London. Epaphroditus Peck had operated from Liverpool, and in 1880 New Haven had an office there at 16 Pitt Street, Cleveland Square, moving to 63 Victoria Street by 1889. Waterbury had an office in Glasgow, at 144–6 Ingram Street, in the early years of the present century.

In order to find out what kind of clocks were being imported into Britain and who was supplying them, three observers have been noting all American clocks seen over a number of years. The results are shown below. Allowance has to be made for those that have been scrapped, and other things being equal, one might expect that the oldest would have gone first, but it is remarkable that no fewer than seventy-five clocks, or eleven per cent, are the product of Chauncey Jerome and therefore made previously to 1855. The forty-one from Jerome & Co are assumed to be from the New Haven Clock Company trading under the Jerome name.

The large number of clocks from the Ansonia Clock Company is predictable, as they did not begin business till 1878 and were active till 1929. Thirteen clocks from the Ansonia Brass and Copper Company, the Ansonia Brass Company and the original Ansonia Clock Company which lasted only from 1850–4 will date from prior to 1878.

During the eight years that they operated, Brewster & Ingrahams were the most important factory in Bristol, but in view of the fact that they entered and left the business comparatively early (1844–52), it is not surprising that fewer of their products remain.

Jerome & Co, E. N. Welch, Waterbury and New Haven all account for forty to fifty examples, but Seth Thomas has half as many again. Adding Jerome & Co and New Haven together gives eighty-five, which slightly beats the Seth Thomas figure. The largest firms together, i.e. Jerome, Ansonia, Welch, Waterbury, Seth Thomas, New Haven and Gilbert contribute seventy-one per cent of the total. The bulk of the activity would have been during the years 1855–1900 as after this time most of the British market was catered for by German factories in the Black Forest and Silesia. The Sessions Clock Company succeeded E. N. Welch in 1903, so their figure relates entirely to the twentieth century. Among the smaller firms are included some who were salesmen only, buying movements from such firms as Jerome and arranging for them to be cased up.

One of the great surprises of the survey is the total of only two clocks from Ingraham. E. Howard of Boston is not represented at all, probably because they made a quality product and the British trade was already supplying the home market with clocks of the more expensive types. The American export to Britain concentrated on the lower-priced clocks. In spite of this, the Terry Clock Company is not represented at all, despite its using a British patent for its luminous dials. The number of balance-controlled clocks is very small indeed, and these clocks are likely to have been casualties comparatively early in their career. It would have been interesting to have compared the sales of these clocks with what the German factories were sending over, but it is most unlikely that this can ever be done.

As far as types of clock are concerned, the thirty-hour OG wins handsomely, with 165 examples. The OOG (which was slightly more expensive) has only sixty-six and the eight day OG and the eight-day Column type which roughly corresponds with it jointly provide fifty-three with five further examples of eight-day OOG.

The Sharp Gothic striking-clock provides thirty-four examples, with seventeen alarms and ten timepieces of the same type. The Cottage style provides a total of forty-one examples: ten strikers, fifteen alarms and sixteen timepieces. The fact that there are only ten Beehives probably means that casualties have been heavy with this type. They are less attractive than some of the other styles in modern eyes, although they were very popular in the mid-nineteenth century. Wall dial-clocks form nearly ten per cent of the total, twenty-six being of the long type and thirty-four of the shorter type. The shorter type includes examples that have been cased in Britain.

Out of the total of 640 clocks in the list, only 513 bore the maker's or vendor's name. In many instances this is due to the fact that papers have been ripped out and that movements did not always have the maker's name or trademark on them. To be a real collectors' item, a clock should have a good legible paper. Naturally a paper in good condition is more desirable, but even torn papers should be preserved if they help to identify the supplier of the clock.

Analysis of clocks by makers

Ansonia. Early firms	13	Smith & Goodrich	1
Ansonia Clock Co	98	J. C. Brown	2
Chauncey Jerome	75	Chauncey Boardman	1
Jerome & Co	41	E. Ingraham & Co	2
New Haven	44	Wm. S. Johnson	3
Seth Thomas	77	Brewster & Brown	2
Waterbury	41	Sperry & Shaw	1
E. N. Welch	46	Birge & Fuller	4
William L. Gilbert	25	Terry & Andrews	1
Brewster & Ingrahams	12	Welch Spring & Co	3
Brewster & Co	3	C & N. Jerome	1
Ithaca	2		——
Pomeroy	1		513
Sessions Clock Co	5	unknown	127
Birge Peck & Co	2		——
Forestville Manufacturing Co	7		640

Analysis of clocks by types

Weight Clocks		Spring Clocks Balance	
OG 30-hour	165	Marine or Locomotive	4
OOG 30-hour	66	Bee	3
OG 8-day	28	Bronze alarm	2
OOG 8-day	5	Joker	3
Column 30-hour	11	Balance TP	1
Column 8-day	25	Winking Eye	2
Wall regulator	4		—
Banjo	1		15
Bronze looking-glass	1		
	—		
	306		

Spring Clocks
Pendulum

Sharp Gothic strike		34	Gilbert and other lancet etc	20
Sharp Gothic alarm		17	Schoolhouse long	26
Sharp Gothic timepiece		10	Schoolhouse short	34
Cottage and other small clocks	Strike	11	circular dial	5
	Alm.	24	Mini OG	5
	TP	20	Royal Bonn Porcelain	4
Beehive		10	Crystal Regulator	2
Walnut		9	Wagon Spring	3
Oak		10	Acorn	1
Marble and imitations		33	Other	17
Mirror and column		7		—
Tivoli etc		17		319

Appendix 3   Makers and Suppliers

Ansonia Clock Company. Theodore Terry, a nephew of Eli, was in partnership with Franklin Andrews at Bristol, Connecticut. In 1850 they were approached by Anson G. Phelps, a financier who had established factories along the Naugatuck River, to remove their plant to his territory which was called 'Ansonia' after his Christian name. The new firm was called 'Ansonia Clock Company'.

Some of the early products incorporate movements marked Terry and Andrews, which were probably on hand when the new factory was established. The Ansonia factory was destroyed by fire in 1854, and the Ansonia Brass and Battery Company which supplied most of the brass for the clock company began to make clock movements to use the brass they manufactured. By 1869 a new corporation was established under the title of 'Ansonia Brass and Copper Company', and in 1877 it was decided to separate the manufacture of clocks into a further new corporation, once again called the 'Ansonia Clock Company'. A new factory was built at New York, where most of the directors resided, but it was burned down in 1880. It was rebuilt in 1881, and by 1883 all the operations from Ansonia had been

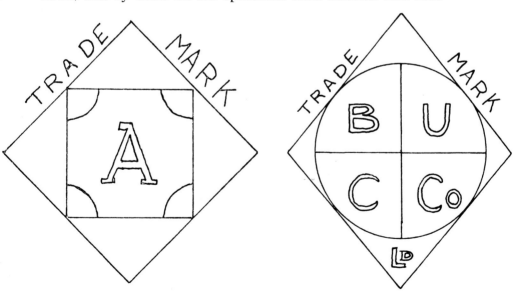

The trademarks of Ansonia and the British United Clock Company.

transferred to it. The firm prospered up to 1914 but after that declined and was wound up in 1929, after which a lot of the machinery was sold to Russia.

British United Clock Company. The BUCC was established at Birmingham in 1885 for manufacturing clocks on the American system. In 1891 they opened a new factory. Their products, which were mostly balance-clocks, received awards at Adelaide in 1887, Melbourne and Sydney in 1888 and Paris in 1889. They went out of business 1909, probably because German products were cheaper.

William L. Gilbert. William L. Gilbert was a schoolteacher who went into the clock business and had many different partners. One of the firms he was in made movements for early Jerome OGs. About 1850 he was established under his own name alone, then in 1866 as the Gilbert Manufacturing Company till 1871, and from then till 1934 the firm was known as the 'William L. Gilbert Clock Company'. After this the firm was known as the 'William L. Gilbert Clock Corporation'. The factory was in Winsted (Winchester), Connecticut. Gilbert was one of the last American firms to send clocks in large quantities to Britain.

Holloway & Co. William Holloway established c. 1842 was 'American Merchant', and Nelson J. Holloway from 1848. They imported American movements and cased them in England. The firm registered a trademark in 1875 which had been in use from 1861. They became agents for Ansonia between 1878 and 1883 but went out of business about this latter year.

The Holloway & Co trademark.

Ingraham. Elias Ingraham worked on his own as a case-maker and then with his brother Andrew and E.C. Brewster as 'Brewster & Ingrahams'. After various changes of partner, the firm became E. Ingraham & Co. Movements were first made in 1865, and later a lot of development work was done on the drum-alarm clock, such as putting the bell inside, using convex glasses and putting the alarm shut-off on the top of the case. The firm still exists.

Jerome. Chauncey Jerome was trained as a carpenter and made cases for Eli Terry. He claimed to have made the first Pillar-and Scroll case for him. He was in partnership with his brother Noble in the 1820s and 1830s, and they developed the cheap brass-movement OG which conquered the British market and began the export of American clocks to Europe. His factory in Bristol was burned in 1845, and he re-established himself in New Haven. He failed in 1855 and later worked for other firms, dying in 1868.

The Jerome and Hew Haven trademarks.

New Haven Clock Company. Chauncey Jerome's nephew Hiram Camp worked with his uncle as superintendent of the movement shop in Bristol until it was destroyed by fire in 1845. Camp then supervised the building of a new factory in New Haven and later worked on his own, supplying Jerome with movements. Demand for movements became greater, and a new Company was formed in 1853 with Hiram Camp as president and the title 'New Haven Clock Company'. When Jerome failed, the New Haven Clock Company took over his factory. The firm was a very large producer but began to go down after 1946 and was liquidated in 1960.

Seth Thomas. Seth Thomas worked for Eli Terry when Terry was beginning his project of mass-producing wooden clock-movements; he eventually bought Terry's shop jointly with Silas Hoadley and later continued on his own. He made various models of Terry's shelf clock under licence and in the 1840s went over to brass movements. Previous to his death in 1859, the firm was made a corporation. Spring-movements were first made about 1861. The factory was located at Plymouth Hollow, but about 1865 the name was changed to 'Thomaston' in honour of the founder. The firm later made turret clocks and also watches. In 1931 it became part of General Time Instruments Corporation and still exists. The movements produced by this firm show sound workmanship.

The Seth Thomas and Waterbury trademarks.

Waterbury Clock Company. This firm was organized at Waterbury, Connecticut, as a branch of the Benedict & Burnham Manufacturing Company, which started as manufacturers of bone and ivory buttons and later of rolled brass. It grew rapidly, and a new factory was required in 1873. The Waterbury Clock Company made most of the popular types of clock and in 1892 began to make watches for

Ingersoll. The famous Waterbury watch was not made by this firm but by an independent Company which got financial help from Benedict & Burnham. Later Ingersoll took over the Waterbury Watch Company which had since changed its name to 'New England Watch Company', but the Ingersoll business itself was acquired by the Waterbury Clock Company in 1922. The Waterbury Clock Company became US Time Corporation in 1944.

E. N. Welch. Elisha N. Welch was a financier rather than a clockmaker and had an interest in many businesses. In the late 1850s he acquired some bankrupt clock-factories in Forestville, Connecticut, including that of J. C. Brown, and in 1864 the E. N. Welch Manufacturing Company was incorporated. In 1868 Welch went into partnership with Solomon. C. Spring under the name of 'Welch, Spring & Co' to make clocks of higher quality than his own factory was producing. This firm lasted till 1884, after which the Welch Company took it over. Certain Welch, Spring models were continued by E. N. Welch, but the firm got into financial difficulties in 1893, and production ceased till 1897. In 1899 the movement-shop was destroyed by fire, and late in the same year the case-shop was also burned. In 1902 members of the Sessions family negotiated to take the firm over, and the new title was 'Sessions Clock Company'.

The E. N. Welch and Western Clock Manufacturing Company trademarks.

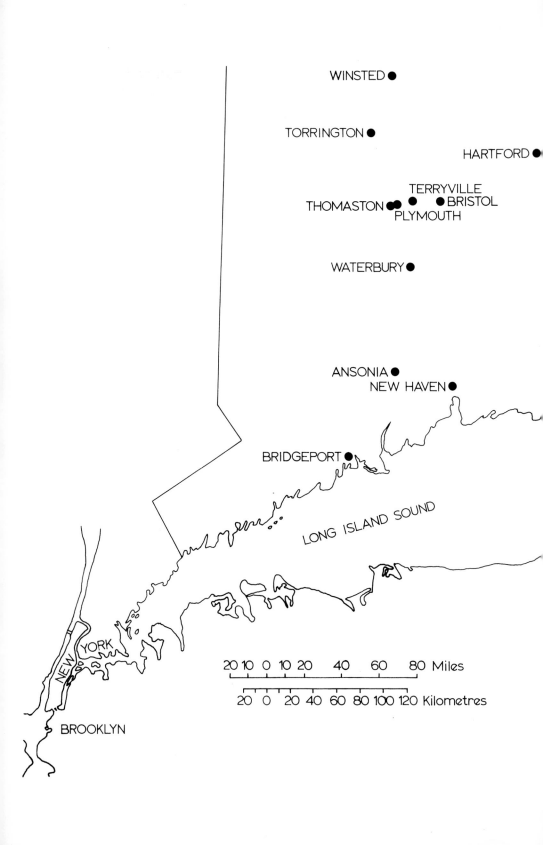

WINSTED ●

TORRINGTON ●

HARTFORD ●●

TERRYVILLE
THOMASTON ●● ● ●BRISTOL
PLYMOUTH

WATERBURY ●

ANSONIA ●
NEW HAVEN ●

BRIDGEPORT ●

LONG ISLAND SOUND

NEW YORK

20 10 0 10 20   40   60   80 Miles

20 0 20 40 60 80 100 120 Kilometres

BROOKLYN

Appendix 4   The State of Connecticut

Connecticut is one of the smallest of the United States, having an area of 5,009 square miles, sixty per cent of which is forested. It is the area in which almost all of the celebrated factories were situated. Connecticut had begun to develop industry in the eighteenth century; as there were rivers to give water-power and as mining for metals was carried on, the State became an ideal place for the development of the clockmaking industry, especially as the forests could provide raw material when movements were made of wood. Forestville is part of Bristol.

The clockmaking towns of Connecticut. (Forestville is part of Bristol.)

Appendix 5   The Ansonia Factory, New York

A description in 1881 from a contemporary encyclopedia.

'A description of the new factory of the Ansonia Clock Co. of Brooklyn, N.Y. will give an idea of the system which is adopted at all the factories in the United States. The floor space occupied amounts to 142,000 square feet and is divided between the main factory, foundry, wood shops, varnish rooms, dry kilns and engine house. The power is furnished by two 250 horse power engines, and all the buildings are lighted with gas made on the grounds. Throughout the entire works at every fifteen feet there is an automatic fire extinguisher, so arranged that when the temperature reaches a given point water will be thrown entirely across the room. More than forty miles of pipe are required to distribute steam, gas and water throughout the works.

'The number of hands employed in May 1881, was 1075, a considerable proportion being boys and girls, and the machinery is to a great degree automatic. The brass for the plates, wheels, etc is rolled in a separate factory, owned by the same Company at Ansonia, Conn., and is prepared to a standard gauge for each required part.

'The plates are first cut to size, and all the brass not required for the support of the train is removed at a single blow of a punching machine, the plumper of which has the shape of the parts to be removed. The plate is then passed to another machine which punches all the holes for posts and pivots except where the holes are less diameter than the thickness of the plate; the position of these holes is marked by this machine, and they are drilled at a separate operation. After the plates are cleaned by being placed with sawdust in large iron holders which revolve at an angle, thus causing the pieces to rub one against another, they are taken to the finishing room, dipped for a moment in boiling acid, thoroughly washed, dried in sawdust, and treated with a very thin coat of lacquer; after which they are spread to dry on large metal tables heated by steam. The plate is then ready to receive the posts or pillars: these are made of heavy wire, which is fed through a straightening machine to an automatic cutter, which cuts them exactly to the required length; then they are fed to a machine for cutting the shoulders, both of

The Ansonia movement of 1882. Left: The front view, showing the French type of pendulum. Right: The rear view, showing the regulating-mechanism.

which are cut at the same moment. The wire is grasped in the centre and held horizontally while two revolving cutters advance, one to each end, and, having been cut to the required depth, which is regulated by a gauge, the wire falls into a receptacle provided, and the operation is repeated. The same method is substantially used in all cases where wire is required for the pivots or posts in any part of the clock. The blanks for the wheels are punched and gutted in the same manner as the plates. A workman takes from 60 to 80 of these blanks and passes a spindle through the centres, care being taken that the blanks are firmly fastened, so that they may not move while being cut. The spindle, with its charge of blanks, is placed in the cutting machine in a horizontal position. The cutters revolve vertically at a right angle to the plane of the intended wheel. Each tooth requires three cuts to complete it—first the saw cut, next the rounding up, and thirdly the finishing cut. The three cutters are upon separate arbors, being placed in exactly the same line, and as the workman with one motion passes the charge of blanks under each cutter in the proper order, the entire tooth is practically cut at the same time. The time required to cut one charge of from 60 to 80 wheels averages about three minutes. The pinion most used in the American clocks is that which is known as the lantern. The wires for the arbors, cut to the required length, are placed upon an inclined plane, down which they pass in regular order, while the planchets for the top and bottom of the pinion (being first punched a little larger than required when finished and also drilled in the centre to receive the arbor) are placed in a hopper.

'The machine being started, one wire falls from the plane and is brought opposite the hole in the planchet; at the same moment a plunger, working horizontally, strikes the wire and drives it the required distance to place the plate in the proper position on the arbor. The top and bottom of the pinion being thus placed, it is next passed to a workman who turns off any surplus metal, and if a shoulder is required anywhere on the arbor, it is turned at the same time. To accomplish this, two cutters are placed in a holder which works in a guide, but is directed by the hands of the workman; this holder is squared in the centre and rounded where the workman grasps it at either end. The cutters, being set at the proper distance, of course make two cuts either in a place parallel with the axis of rotation or at right angles to it, as may be desired. Two other cutters are placed in the same holder at 90° from the first, so that four cuts may be made by revolving the holder one quarter of a revolution. The heads, now being finished, are drilled to receive the wires which constitute the leaves. The operation is mostly performed by girls. An arbor bearing the top and bottom of the pinion is grasped horizontally in a clutch which is connected with a plate having as many holes as leaves are required in the pinion; this part is then advanced against a drill also working horizontally and revolving at a speed of about 18,000 revolutions a minute; the hole is drilled through the head of the pinion and partly through the bottom, accuracy in depth being secured by a stop. The sliding holder is withdrawn and turned to the next hole in the plate, when the operation is repeated until the proper number of holes is drilled.

'The blanks are then ready to receive the leaves: these are of steel wire, which is polished and cut to the required length, a trifle less than the depth of the holes already drilled. Girls then drop these small wires with astonishing rapidity into the holes; they are passed directly to another series of hands, who by a few light blows of a riveting hammer worked by the foot close the holes over the ends of the leaves and the pinion is finished.

'The main springs (weights being very little used at present except where great accuracy to time is desired) are coiled and tempered as any other spring would be, and each spring is then separately tested for strength in the following manner: one end of the spring is fastened firmly to a holder, and the other is connected to an arbor which is allowed to revolve; suspended from this arbor is a weight which the spring in uncoiling is required to raise to a given height. Failing to do this it is rejected. All the smaller parts of the clock, such as the cocks, lever etc, are made by automatic machinery. A considerable proportion of the clocks at present made are of the small lever style, going in any position. The manner of making the balance wheel is interesting. A brass tube slightly larger than the required diameter of the wheel is placed in a lathe, and the workman turns out the inside to a gauge, and afterwards, with another cutter on the same lathe, the outside circumference of the wheel. A cutter working vertically then cuts the circle from the tube, the cutter being so shaped as to finish the inside surface at the same time. One man will turn three thousand balances per day. The next process is to drill the holes for the arms. The rings of metal are placed singly upon a vertical hub made so as to revolve one third of a revolution at each movement; this hub moves upon a horizontal plane and brings the part to be drilled against a fast revolving drill. One hole being drilled the hub is drawn back, turned 120°, and the operation repeated; the small steel wires are then inserted to connect the periphery with the collet which fits the balance arbor.

'The making of hair springs requires more skill on the part of the workman than almost any other portion of the clock. The steel is rolled to the proper thickness and cut the desired width. The operative then takes four of these strips and places one on top of the other, being careful that the ends are exactly even. He then puts one end in a slit in an arbor similar to those used by watchmakers to wind mainsprings. This arbor is then slowly and carefully revolved until the strips are almost wound inside of a small box like a shallow mainspring barrel of a watch: just before the winding is completed another strip of steel is inserted of sufficient length to exactly fill the box, thus preventing the coils from expanding. A small metal table heated by a gas flame is placed on the workbench immediately before the workman, who, as soon as the spring is wound removes it, still in the box, and places it upon this heated table to temper, watching the process carefully and judging by the colour when the springs should be removed. The completed hairspring is then fastened to the collet by inserting the end of the interior coil in a diagonal cut in the collet which cut is closed by a light blow with a hammer.

'As the various parts are finished they are taken to the store room and placed in separate bins until wanted. The work of putting the clock together is done by girls. The lower plate having been placed in a clutch on the work table, the various parts are taken from the different boxes, put into their proper position, and the upper plate put on and fastened either by screws in the posts or by pins. The rapidity with which this operation is performed is wonderful: each girl is expected to put about 400 clocks together in a working day.

'From the setter up the movement now passes to the adjuster, who inserts the balance wheel and approximately regulates it. The men to whom is entrusted this operation are placed by twos in separate rooms. A clock with the same calculations as those to be regulated is placed in a position where the vibrations can be distinctly heard. After putting in the balance wheel the workmen compare the vibrations for a few seconds and either shorten or lengthen the hairspring as the case may require until the clock under regulation makes forty synchronous vibrations with the standard, when it is considered regulated; and so expert do these adjusters become in detecting a difference in vibrations that a movement seldom varies three minutes in twenty four hours. If the variation reaches this amount it is returned to the person who adjusted it and is charged against his work.

'The striking part of an American clock is totally different from that of a French or English clock, both the locking and striking part being between the plates instead of under the dial; the rack and snail are entirely discarded, and in place a wheel is substituted having twelve deep cuts, into one of which a wire arm falls after the striking of each hour. Between these deep cuts ratchet shaped teeth are cut on the periphery of the wheel, in number in accordance with the strokes required for the several hours. This wheel is placed on the same arbor with the wheel bearing the lifting pins for raising the hammer, but is held in its place by a spring allowing a free motion separate from the wheel with which it is placed. Projecting from the pinion which meshes into the wheel bearing the lifting pins is a pin which upon each revolution of the pinion catches one of the ratchet shaped teeth before described and moves it forward. As the number of leaves in this pinion is the same as the number of teeth between the lifting pins, it follows that at each stroke of the hammer the count wheel is advanced one tooth, and when one of the deep cuts is reached the arm falls and completes the locking. To effect the warning and locking an ingenious system of light wire rods bent in dies to the proper shape renders the parts very inexpensive to construct.

'The manufacture of the cases is a very important branch of a clock factory. For many years the only forms of case known were the large square and the sharp pointed Gothic, but as the popular taste improved these passed away, and the success of a manufacturer is now due as much to the style of his cases as the quality of the movements. For the wooden cases the wood is first dried in large kilns, being so stacked that the heated air will pass over and under each piece; as the air becomes filled with the moisture from the wood, it is drawn off in such a way that a constant circulation is maintained.

'The smoothing of the wood is very expenditiously and effectively done. Instead of the ordinary method of sand papering by hand, drums 5 feet in diameter, driven by steam, are covered with a coating of sand, and the part to be smoothed is held for a moment against the face of the drum, and all inequalities are thus removed. When it is required to sand paper a moulding the reverse of the moulding is cut upon the drum, covered with sand, and when the moulding is brought in contact with this surface the polishing is done very thoroughly.

'Within the last few years iron cases in imitation of the French marble clocks have been in great demand; these are so cast as to secure as good a surface as possible. They then receive three coats of lacquer, and after the application of each coat except the last they are baked in large ovens for four hours. When the finishing coat is applied they are left in the ovens for twelve hours. After the movements are put in the cases they are again run for twenty four hours, and then packed for shipment.

'The amount of capital invested in this industry is, as nearly as can be ascertained $3,250,000; operatives employed 3,500, annual amount of wages $1,500,000; annual production in value $5,000,000; number of clocks produced annually 1,750,000. About one third of the entire production is exported.'

Appendix 6 Sam Slick

The term 'Sam Slick' is often applied to early American clocks, and some notes on this may be of interest. The character Samuel Slick of Slickville, Onion County, Connecticut, was an American clock-pedlar who operated in Canada, and the book in which he appears is entitled *The Clockmaker*. It consists of a number of chapters, mostly separate stories about the central character. It was written by Thomas Chandler Haliburton (1796–1865), a Canadian humorist, lawyer and judge who retired to Britain in 1856.

It is suggested that Slick painted and gilded the cases of the clocks that he sold, which was most unlikely, for during the 1830s, when the stories take place, making and selling clocks were two separate activities. There is not much of horological interest in the book, which corresponds to such works as Dickens' *Sketches by Boz*, published in Britain, *Sketches of Life and Character* by T. S. Arthur, published in the USA, and *Camera Obscura* by Nicholas Beets, published in Holland. All these books appeared within a few years of each other.

The main theme of the stories is Slick's smartness. He leaves a clock with a family to mind till he calls for it again, knowing that by the time he returns they will have got too used to it to let it go – hence another sale for him. The following extracts are those which relate to selling and making clocks, but perhaps it is best not to take them too seriously. It is important to remember that the book was written before the financial crisis of 1837 and that Slick's business was exclusively in wooden-movement clocks.

'A Yankee clockmaker sells clocks warranted to run from July to Eternity stoppages included.'

'By selling Yankee clocks in Canada it would drain all the money out of Canada into USA.'

'They don't make good ones any more for they calculate 'em for shipping and not for home use.'

'A particularly handsome one, copald and gilt superior.'

'He got the most inferior article I had and I just doubled the price on him.'

'The clock struck seven, a wooden clock to which Mr Slick looked with evident satisfaction as proof of his previous acquaintance.'

'My first tour in the clock trade was up Canada way and I was the first ever went up the Huron with clocks.'

'They had cheats enough in Nova Scotia without having Yankee clockmakers to put new wrinkles on their horns.'

'You are a considerable judge of painting seein' that you do bronzing and gilding so beautiful.'

'A knowledge of latten has been of great service to me in the clock trade. . . . You mix up calamine and copper and it makes a brass as near like gold as one pea is to another.'

'Like Slick's clocks. All gilded and varnished outside and soft wood within.'

'In my little back studio to Slickville with coat off, apron on and sleeves up as busy as a bee a bronzin' and a gildin' of a clock case.'

'Landscape on the right with a great white two story house.' (Tablet design)

'When I was down in Rhode Island learning bronzing, gilding and sketching for the clock business.'

'"I've been here before" said Mr Slick, pointing to a wooden clock in the corner of the room.'

'The clock trade is now done in this province. There's an end to that. You've put a toggle into that chain. You couldn't give 'em away now a'most.' (Sam Slick reprimands the author for having published his first book giving the secrets of the trade away.)

'All goods in Canada are English except a few thousand wooden clocks I introduced here to let em know when grog time of day comes.'

'As dumb as a wooden clock two years old.'

Index

(Types of clock in bold lettering)

A
Acorn, 48, 162, 163
Alarm Work, 6, 34, 51
Ansonia Brass and Battery Co., 53, 191
Ansonia Brass and Copper Co., 187, 191
Ansonia Clock Co., 54, 80, 81, 84, 99, 101, 102, 115, 117, 161, 164, 165, 166, 168, 171, 188, 198
Antiquarian Horological Society, 160
Arabic Figures, 9, 68
Arbor, 123
Atwood, Anson, 30
Austria, 20

B
Baby Ben, 83
Badische Uhrenfabrik, 110
Baird, E. P., 103, 164
Balmain, William, 76
Banjo, 6, 11, 18, 19, 39, 40, 47, 51, 120, 161, 162, 163, 166
Barnes, William B., 74
Barrel, 38
Bee, 82, 118
Beehive, 43, 47, 50, 53, 59, 145
Benedict and Burnham, 194, 195
Berliner, 96, 166
Biddle and Mumford (Gears) Ltd, 165
Big Ben, 83
Birge and Fuller, 41, 48
Birge Peck and Co., 27, 68
Birmingham, 8
Black Forest, 9, 18, 21, 82, 89, 102, 105, 106, 126, 188
Boardman and Wells, 46, 48
Bostwick and Burgess, 102
Brass, 24, 41

Brewster, E. C., 42, 47, 53
  E. C. and Co., 30
  E. C. and Son, 30
  and Ingrahams, 30, 31, 44, 48, 54, 68, 186, 188
  single pin strike, 29, 55, 134
Briggs, J. C., 100, 166, 171
Bristol, Connecticut, 10, 29, 40
British Horological Institute, 160
British Jerome Co., 187
British Library, 96
British Museum, 48
British United Clock Co., 118, 192
Brocot suspension, 56
Bronze Looking-Glass clock, 16, 17, 121
Brown, J. C., 48, 60
Burnap, Daniel, 3, 4, 9
Bushes, 130

C
Caledonian, 119
Cam, 25
Cambridge Chimes, 120
Camp, Hiram, 29, 193
Canada, 16, 204, 205
Carriage clock, 72, 84, 118
Case-on-case, 4, 8, 11, 18, 20, 48, 51
Civil War, 53, 77
Clausen, A. C., 101
Cleaning, 132
Clock Trade Enterprises, 165
Columbus, 102, 166
Connecticut, 9, 16, 18, 24, 53, 159, 197
Cottage, 50
Cottey, Abel, 2
Count wheel, 13, 16, 25, 27, 29, 31, 46
Crane, Aaron D., 99
Crystal regulator, 58, 66
Customs, 26

D
Davies, H. J., 99
Davis striking, 29
Dial, 6, 8, 32, 150 et seq.
Doric, 54, 59
Dresden, 67
Dunbar, Edward L., 48, 50, 74

E
Eagle, American, 8
Eagle Manufacturing Co., 113
Empire-style clock, 32, 170
English dial, 63
Escapement, 71
Escapement, lever, 72, 74
Essex, 67
Extra bushed, 33

F
Factory clocks, 21
Fashion, 94
Fattorini, 117
Fitch, Eugene L., 102
Fly, 130
Foliot, 71
Forestville Manufacturing Co., 162
France, 9
Francis and Loutrel, 35
Franklin clock, 87
Freeswinger, 96
French clocks, 51, 56
Freunde Alter Uhren, 160
Fusee, 38

G
Gale, Daniel J., 93
Georgia, 2
Geer, Elihu, 34
German clockmakers, 18
Germany, 20
Gila, 63
Gilbert, William L., 26, 54, 65, 68, 95, 192
Gingerbread, 61
Girandole, 8
Gnat, 118
Gong, 106

Grain, 125
Grandfather, 119
Grandmother, 6, 8
Grant, Zelotes S., 26, 28
Grieg, John S., 97
Grimthorpe, 140
Groaner, 88, 127

H
Haas, Philipp, 68, 109
HAC, HAU, 108
Half-hour strike, 57
Haliburton, Thomas Chandler, 204
Hamburg, 27
Hamilton Watch Co., 102
Hands, 19, 154
Harland, Thomas, 3
Harrison, John, 125
Hoadley, Silas, 10, 87, 127, 164
Holloway and Co., 36, 68, 112, 187, 192
Howard Co., 8, 89, 94, 119, 120, 159, 166
HPF, 32

I
Ignatz, 101, 166
Ingersoll, 80, 195
Ingraham, Andrew, 44
    Brothers, 43, 46
    Elias, 44, 53
    E. and Co., 60, 63, 68, 79
Ithaca Calendar Clock Co., 90
Ives, Joseph, 16, 27, 40, 54, 89
Ives, Joseph Shaylor, 41

J
Japan, 111, 159
Jefferson embargo, 9
Jerome, Chauncey, 23, 26, 28, 29, 47, 48, 49, 50, 63, 68, 88, 105, 192
    Noble, 25, 27, 28, 41, 47, 88
    and Co., 50, 119, 164, 187, 188
Jeromes and Co., 26
Joker, 85
Junghans, 105, 108

K
Kent, 67
Kirk, Charles, 30, 164
Kroeber, Florence, 97, 164

L
Lancaster County, Pennsylvania,
    17
Lancet, 43, 68
Lantern clock, 2
Lantern pinion, 131
Leipsic, 67
Lewis, B. B., 90, 94
Liverpool, 27
Long Case clock, 2, 6, 16, 18, 19,
    162
Lyre clock, 8

M
Mainspring, 38 *et seq.*, 141
Maltese Cross hands, 31
Maranville, 94
Marble, 145
Marine or Locomotive, 74, 165
Massachusetts, 4
Metal, shortage of, 4
Mirror clock, 6
Motion work, 11
Museums:
    American Clock and Watch,
        160
    American Museum,Bath, 163
    Atwood, Seth, 162
    British Museum, 163
    Furtwangen, 164
    Henry Ford, 162
    Ilfracombe, 164
    Illinois State Museum,
        Springfield, 162
    Kendal, 164
    Kirkstall Abbey, 163
    NAWCC, Columbia,
        Pennsylvania, 162
    Old Sturbridge Village, 162
    Oxford, 164
    Royal Albert, Exeter, 2
    Schoonhoven, 164

    Smithsonian Institution,
        Washington DC, 162
    Tiverton, 164
    Tiverton Castle, 164
    Victoria and Albert, 163
    Welsh Folk Museum, 164
    Wuppertal, 165

N
Napoleon, 10
NAWCC, 159, 162
New Hampshire, 6, 47
New Haven Clock Co., 30, 35, 49,
    50, 65, 68, 79, 80, 95, 99, 115,
    119, 187, 188, 193
North family, 88
Northbury, 9
Norwich, Connecticut, 3

O
Oaks, 61, 66, 164, 170
Octagon, 50
OG, 23 *et seq.*, 42, 43, 46, 47, 59,
    105, 127 *et seq.*, 161, 164, 171
OG Gothic, 47
Oiling, 33
OOG, 23 *et seq.*, 164

P
Pallets, 136
Papers, 34, 181 *et seq.*
Parker Clock Co., 82
Patti, 61, 110, 166
Peck, Epaphroditus, 186, 187
Pendulum, 138
Pennsylvania, 18
Pewter, 11
Piecrust, 48
Pillar and scroll, 13, 16, 40, 87,
    162, 166, 168, 170
Pivots, 130
Plato, 102, 166
Plymouth, 9
Plymouth Hollow, 10, 34, 194
Porter, Edward and Levi, 10
Prentiss Calendar and Time Co.,
    94

Previosa, 108
Pulleys, 147
Putnam, 121

R
Rack and Snail Striking, 13, 29
Rat Trap Striking, 6
Ray and Ingraham, 43, 44
Regulation, 34
Richmond Virginia, 24
Ripple, 48
Roberts, Gideon, 10
Roller Pinions, 40, 54
Round Gothic, 43, 44, 48
Roxbury, 6
Royal Bonn Porcelain, 66, 164

S
St Louis Clock and Silverware Co.,
    66, 96, 121
Schoolhouse, 65, 166, 170
Sessions, 188, 195
Sharp Gothic, 44, 46, 48, 50, 51,
    59, 67, 161, 164
Shelf clock, 13, 16, 20, 24, 27,
    37, 42
Sidewhiskers, 61
Silesia, 188
Southern Calendar Clock Co., 94
Sperry and Shaw, 26
Spring, Solomon C., 60, 195
Springs, brass, 41, 42, 46
        steel, 38 *et seq.*, 141
Stars and Stripes, 8
Steel plates, 89
Sting, 79
Suffolk, 67
Swinger, 101, 168

T
Teeth, 133
Terry, Eli, 3, 9, 13, 25, 28, 41, 46,
    73, 105, 111, 126, 166, 168,
    170
        Silas B., 47, 48, 73
        and Andrews, 191
        Clock Co., 76

Testing Rod, 39
Teutonia, 108
Thomas, Aaron, 50
Thomas, Seth, 10, 16, 28, 30, 31,
    34, 35, 50, 51, 53, 65, 68, 75,
    79, 85, 90, 95, 104, 108, 111,
    115, 159, 162, 187, 188, 194
Thomaston, 34, 194
Tiger, 23
Tivoli, 60
Tools, 122
Traveler, 84
Tunis, 60

V
Veneer, 24, 37
Venetian, 54, 59, 98, 108
Verdi, 65
Vienna regulator, 65, 67, 95, 108,
    166

W
Wagon spring, 40, 48, 162
Walnuts, 58
Waltham Clock Co., 120
War of 1812, 9
War of Independence, 3
Waterbury Clock Co., 30, 33, 58,
    80, 95, 104, 120, 156, 187,
    194
Welch, E. N., 48, 65, 75, 80, 94,
    99, 115, 162, 187, 188, 195
Welch Spring and Co., 60, 65, 91,
    93, 94, 110, 159, 166
Western Clock Manufacturing Co.,
    80, 83
Westminster chimes, 120
Whitney, Eli, 10
Willard, Simon, 6, 11, 19, 162
Wood, 123
Wood's Patent Alarm, 164
Wooden clock, 9, 10, 19, 24, 42

Y
Yankee Pedlars, 18
Yale Clock Co., 102